GW00535895

The Internet and Web Authoring

Fionnuala Nicholson and Jacqueline Dempsey

Gill & Macmillan

Gill & Macmillan
Hume Avenue
Park West
Dublin 12
with associated companies throughout the world www.gillmacmillan.ie

© Fionnuala Nicholson and Jacqueline Dempsey 2011

978 07171 4983 4

Print origination in Ireland by Carole Lynch
Printed by GraphyCems, Spain

Disclaimer

Photograph © Cern/Science Photo Library, page 20.

The Internet and Web Authoring

Contents

Acknowledgments

We would like to thank all our students whose generous response greatly contributed to the success of this book in the teaching environment.

A special thank you to our colleagues, in particular Donnchadh for his kind support and continued encouragement.

Finally, many thanks to our families for their patience and understanding.

Introduction

This book covers the requirements of FETAC Level 5 Modules for The Internet and for Web Authoring.

The support material on www.gillmacmillan.ie contains specific exercises for the Web Publishing section of the Internet Module C20168, which are also suitable for the Web Authoring Module C20148. You will need to type 'The Internet and Web Authoring' into the search tool on gillmacmillan.ie to access this material.

It is our hope that you will enjoy using this manual and the support material.

Both authors teach Computer Studies and the material in this book has been developed through a series of successful tutorials already given to students.

The History and Structure of the Internet

Historical Development of the Internet

The Internet is the global network of interconnected computers. It is defined by its own set of unique rules or protocols, particularly the TCP/IP suite of protocols, and particularly by the fact that it is a packet switched network.

Emergence of the Internet

The idea of a global network was introduced by J. C. K. Licklider of MIT (Massachusetts Institute of Technology) in August 1962. He envisaged a situation where interconnected networked computers could talk to each other globally, and share programs and information with each other.[1]

ARPANET Project

The ARPANET (Advanced Research Projects Agency Network) was developed by the IPTO (Information Processing Techniques Office) under the sponsorship of DARPA (the Defence Advanced Research Projects Agency). Its motivation was prompted, among other things, by the launch of Sputnik 1 by the Soviet Union in 1957.

The ARPANET's project objective was to develop a network communications technology where computers and networks could connect and talk to each other, share data and have the capacity to function even if one of the networks was damaged.

In 1963 a universal standard code was developed which allowed machines 'from different manufacturers to exchange data'.[2] This was known as the ASCII (American Standard Code for Information Interchange) code.

With ARPA funding, the first long-distance network connection occurred in 1965, when Larry Roberts and Thomas Marill connected the TX-2 computer at MIT's Lincoln Laboratory in Massachusetts to the Q-32 computer in Santa Monica, California.[3] It became apparent that using the existing telephone system for transmitting information was too slow. The necessity of packet switching was suggested by Leonard Kleinrock at MIT.

Packet switching can be explained by comparing it with the existing telephone system, widely known now as the Plain Old Telephone Service (POTS). Here, for a conversation to take place, a continuous connection has to be made between the two parties, whether this is a voice conversation or two modems sending and receiving data. In comparison, a packet switched network transmits packets of data. These packets can follow different routes. The computer receiving the packets is able to reassemble the stream of data and ask for re-transmission of damaged or missing data. The ARPANET became the first network to use packet switching. The first connection between two computers on the ARPANET occurred in the autumn of 1969.

At this time, the ARPANET was still a very small network limited to the academic, medical and industrial/military sectors. Nevertheless, important developments were made: in particular, the concept that packet switched networks worked was proved. The Network Control and File Transfer Protocols (NCP and FTP) were developed.

Timeline

- 1971 – Intel developed the first microchip, the necessary precursor to all the electronic gadgetry we find indispensable today.
- 1972 – Ray Tomlinson wrote a program to allow transmission of electronic mail over the ARPANET. He initiated the now familiar 'name@host' form of e-mail address.
- Mid-1970s – hobbyists began building their own computers from kits. This small but enthusiastic band of amateurs eventually began to avail of some aspects of the ARPANET which allowed them to play games against people in other cities and to connect to bulletin boards.
- 1977 – Apple began selling its Apple II home computer.
- 1979 – Usenet was introduced. It still exists and is a separate part of the Internet. It is a distributed system: that is, its postings are interchanged between hosts on a regular basis. It features threaded discussion groups to which anyone one can subscribe.
- 1981 – IBM launched their personal computer, the predecessor of all today's PCs.
- 1985 – Windows 1.0 operating system arrived on the scene. It included a small number of desktop applications, including a notepad, a clock, a calculator and a calendar.

- 1990 – Windows 3.0 was introduced. It had better icons, a file manager, a print manager, and a program manager. It was the first successful commercial version of Windows.
- 1993 – Windows NT (New Technology) was introduced: it had a full 32-bit operating system and dropped the link with DOS.
- 1995 – Microsoft released the first cross-platform browser (Internet Explorer 2.0).
- 1996 – Windows NT was upgraded to Windows NT 4.0.
- 1998 – Windows 98 was released. Since then Microsoft have brought out a number of new versions of Windows, the latest being Windows 7, released in 2009.

Development of the TCP/IP Protocols

The Internet is a man-made construct and functions with high reliability because of the underlying rules, or protocols, to which every computer accessing the Web must conform. It is not the purpose of this book to study these rules but mention is made of two of the most important, namely TCP and IP.

Although the Network Control Protocol (NCP) allowed host computers to talk to each other within a network, it was realised that the NCP was very limited in what it could do. The solution was the development of the crucial Transmission Control Protocol/Internet Protocol (TCP/IP) protocol suite.

These protocols are the rules governing how computers connect and communicate with each other on the Internet. The co-designers of the TCP/IP Protocol were Vinton Cerf and Robert Kahn.

'In December of 1974, Dr Vinton Cerf, with Stanford graduate students Yogen Dalal and Carl Sunshine, published the first technical specification of TCP/IP as an Internet Experiment Note RFC (refer for comment) 675.'[4] RFC 675 is available for viewing at the following web address: http://www.tools.ietf.org/html/rfc675. Interestingly, their design included a 32-bit IP address. Dr Kahn had considered the possibility of having networks communicating with each other independent of 'individual hardware and software configuration'.[5] So, he set four goals for what would become the Transmission Control Protocol:

- **Network connectivity**. Any network could connect to another network through a gateway.
- **Distribution**. There would be no central network administration or control.
- **Error recovery**. Lost packets would be retransmitted.
- **Black box design**. No internal changes would have to be made to a computer to connect it to the network.[6]

Later, the 'Transmission Control Protocol design was layered into two protocols' – TCP/IP. TCP/IP is the primary protocol that governs the Internet.

- The TCP manages the disassembling and reassembling of data packets, which are then brought back to their original data format. It is also responsible for the retransmission of lost packets. TCP communicates with the host application on one computer and the host application on another computer on a network or networks. (Definition of TCP from SearchNetworking.com http://search networking/ techtarget.com/sDefinition/0,,sid7_gci214173,00.html.)
- Internet Protocol (IP) is the protocol that is responsible for the address component of data packets, which are sent from one computer to another computer over a network or networks.

The TCP/IP protocol was formally adopted as the standard for the ARPANET in 1983. A computer on one network wanting to connect with a computer on the ARPANET had to use this protocol.

The EUNET (European Network) connected to the ARPANET in 1989. Ireland was linked to the Internet backbone in 1990.

In 1980, the National Science Foundation (NSF) 'funded the development of CSNET [Computer Science Network], to link computer science departments in America not connected to the Arpanet'.[8] Subsequently, NSFNET was established, and in 1991 the NSFNET backbone was upgraded to T3, or 45 Mbps.

Also in 1991 NSF had changed its AUP (acceptable use policy): this meant that the Internet was no longer restricted to the research community, computer developers and the academic world – it had now become accessible to anyone, providing they had a computer and an Internet connection.

In 1990, the ARPANET was retired, and a number of university computers connected to the ARPARNET now moved to the NSFNET.[9] Some of the services offered by the APRANET had included mail, file transfer and remote log on Telnet.

Throughout the 1980s private companies and government agencies had set up their own networks, for example CompuServe and AOL. Networks now began to interconnect and the scene was set for the rapid expansion of the Internet.

Development of the World Wide Web

The World Wide Web (WWW) is possibly the foremost contributing factor responsible for the explosion of the Internet. As mentioned above, the Internet is a network of networked computers.

The Web links together pages, data and resources which are held on Web servers all over the world. You navigate around the Web by entering a Web address – the address of a particular website, known as a URL (Uniform Resource Locator) – in your browser window. Your browser will then locate the website and you can navigate from one page to another by clicking on the hyperlinks. A browser, which is a client application, receives, interprets and displays web pages.

How it All Began

The World Wide Web was introduced by Tim Berners-Lee. His story of how the Web evolved is told in his publication, *Weaving the Web: The Original Design and Ultimate Destiny of the World Wide Web by its Inventor*.

While working at CERN (Organisation Européenne pour la Recherche Nucléaire), in Geneva, Switzerland, Tim Berners-Lee had been considering how he might link research documents across computers. He wanted to share research findings and he wanted this sharing to be interactive.

In 1989 he produced *Information Management: A Proposal* (Tim Berners-Lee, CERN, March 1989.[10] This document is available to view at http://www.w3.org/History.) Here he introduced the idea of a protocol that could transmit and link documents across operating systems and across the Internet. This is known as the HTTP (HyperText Transfer Protocol).

- **HTTP** sits on top of the TCP/IP protocol, which is used to connect to Web servers. HTTP is a request/response system: it delivers to your browser web pages that have been requested.
- **HyperText** was a concept already in existence: it had been mentioned by Vanevar Bush in 1945 – before computers were invented – and by Ted Nelson and Doug Engelbart in 1960. Hypertext allows you to jump from link to link in a non-linear way.
- **HTML** (HyperText Markup Language) was developed to write web pages so that computers with different operating systems could communicate with each other.

First Web Server

Tim Berners-Lee used a NeXT computer as a Web server. It was the first Web server, hypermedia browser and Web editor.

First Website

The first website was put on line on 6 August 1991. The first Web surfer was Robert Cailliau, a Belgian computer scientist who had collaborated with Tim Berners-Lee on the World Wide Web project.[11] In April 1993 CERN announced that the World Wide Web would be free to everyone.

It is worth noting that Tim Berners-Lee, who invented the 'Web', has consistently refused to sell it – he wants it to be an open forum and not in the ownership of any particular organisation or nation. He had vision and he knew that the WWW needed control and organisation.

It was for this reason that in 1994 he established a consortium, known as the World Wide Web Consortium (or W3C), membership of which is open to educational bodies, organisations, and commercial and government entities. Tim Berners-Lee states that 'W3C members work together to design Web technologies that build upon its universality, giving the world the power to enhance communication and commerce for anyone, anywhere, anytime and using any device.' Membership details are available at http://www.w3.org/Consortium/membership. Membership is not open to private individuals.

In 1993, Marc Andreesen and his team (which included Eric Bina) at the National Center for Super Computing at the University of Illinois developed a graphic interface browser which was named 'Mosaic'. Mosaic was easy to use, and allowed images to be displayed in line with text within pages – until then you had to link an image which had to be displayed on a different page. The design also included additional HTML tags.

Some of the major browsers available today include:

- Microsoft Internet Explorer
- Google Chrome
- Mozilla Firefox
- Apple Safari
- Opera.

It is reported that, of the world population of 6.8 billion, 1.73 billion people are Internet users: that's approximately 26% of the global population.

Structure of the Internet – Ownership, Administration and Funding

As with everything related to computers, the Internet has a physical/hardware element and a software/rules element. The hardware element stretches from the client PC in the home or office through the cabling and other infrastructure taking signals to an ISP and thence to the Internet backbone and ultimately to the server providing the web page or to another ISP for receipt of an e-mail message.

Private individuals connect to the Internet through their Internet Service Provider (ISP). Their ISP in turn connects with other higher-level networks. These networks use trunk routes which are usually owned by governments or commercial organisations. They carry data across oceans and continents.

The trunk routes are the backbone of the Internet. They offer high speed, and they may use fibre optic cabling. These networks are connected at Internet Exchange Points (IXPs).[12]

Ownership

No one actually owns the Internet. It is not under the control of any one government or organisation. The elements of its physical infrastructure – networks, cables, routers, etc. – are owned by organisations: government bodies, ISPs and commercial institutions.

Administration

How does the Internet function if no one government or organisation actually owns it? It is organised by consensus, with the co-operation of international bodies who work together under the mantle of the Internet Society (ISOC), whose board of trustees are concerned about the Internet and its impact on society. ISOC is a non-profit-making organisation with offices in Washington and Geneva and chapters all over the world. There are over 80 organisations involved. Some of the most relevant bodies in terms of influence and power are listed on the following page.

ISOC's mission statement is: 'To assure the open development, evolution and use of the Internet for the benefit of all people throughout the world.' It 'facilitates open development of standards, protocols, administration and the technical infrastructure of the Internet'.[13]

The society was founded in 1992 and was awarded the right to manage the .org domain in 2002. Membership is open to any individual.

Some of the groups associated with ISOC are:

- **Internet Architecture Board (IAB)** – 'The IAB is chartered both as a committee of the Internet Engineering Task Force [IETF] and as an advisory body of the Internet Society.'[14] IAB offers guidance and advice to the ISOC on the architectural procedures and the technologies used on the Internet. It is responsible for the editorial management and publication of the Request for Comments (RFC) document series.
- **Internet Engineering Task Force (IETF)**. The goal of the IETF is to make the Internet work better. In its mission statement it says that it aims to 'make the Internet work better by producing high quality, relevant technical documents that influence the way people design, use, and manage the Internet'.
- **Internet Research Task Force (IRTF)**. Its mission is: 'To promote research of importance to the evolution of the future Internet by creating focused, long-term and small Research Groups working on topics related to Internet protocols, applications, architecture and technology.'[15]
- **Internet Assigned Numbers Authority (IANA)**: responsible for the global co-ordination of the DNS Root, IP addressing, and other Internet protocol resources.[16]

Funding

ISOC receives funding from the following sources:

- organisation members' contributions (including platinum sponsorships)
- individual member dues and donations
- sponsorships for ISOC events
- contribution of excess net assets from the Public Interest Registry.[17]

Assessment of the Internet as a New Communications Medium

The Internet was originally conceived as a means of sharing knowledge, research papers and information. As it evolved it became obvious that an overall organisational structure was required.

As we are already aware, the Internet had by 1996 moved beyond the realms of academia, and millions and millions of people were surfing the Web. Desktop computers, which were known as personal computers (PCs), had become available and affordable. Organisations such as IBM and Microsoft had designed applications that were 'user friendly'. The Netscape browser had gone public and Microsoft had introduced Internet Explorer and had bundled it with its Windows operating system. Today newspapers are available online; music, books and videos can be downloaded and viewed on desktop or laptop computers. Radio stations are streamed.

The Internet Society was established to oversee the development of the Internet in a structured manner. Concepts such as ethics, intellectual property, privacy and content had to be addressed. Some of these issues had already been debated with the invention of earlier technologies, for example telegrams, telephone, newspapers, films, radio and television. But here lies the difference: information is now available globally in real time. Reaction to world events can be swift. Security issues have to be considered and implemented.

Undoubtedly, the Internet has changed communication: there is openness, and individuals have access to the latest news, ideas, research and scientific findings and, more important, have the power and willingness to publish their views and opinions on the Web. But this new freedom of expression can also be used to turn communities against each other.

Communications

Personal

Today you can communicate with your friends in real time using Internet technologies such as:

- Instant Messaging (IM), which consists of sending instant text messages from one computer to another.
- Blogs (Web journals), which you can use to express your views.
- Twitter – to post a tweet to your Twitter account (you will then have tweeted). The maximum number of characters per 'tweet' (message) is 140 characters.
- E-mail (electronic mail) messages – faster and cheaper than using the normal postal system.
- Voice over Internet Protocol (VoIP), a technology that allows you to make computer-to-computer calls, for example Skype and Google Talk.
- Social networking sites, which are among the most popular sites on the Internet, for example:
  — Facebook
  — Bebo
  — YouTube (used to share and view videos)
  — Flickr (used to share photographs and videos).

Professional Training and Development

Use of the Internet as a resource for personal and professional training and development has become part of today's world. University students are expected to be familiar with the Internet and to be able to send and receive e-mails and to access publications online.

A number of institutions offer courses which are delivered entirely online, for example:

- National University of Ireland in Galway – an online course on Irish Studies
- Trinity College Dublin – an iTunes U portal where podcasts and videos/movies can be downloaded
- a number of leading American universities (Berkeley, MIT, Stanford and Yale) have opened some of their courses and lectures to the public. These lectures can, of course, be downloaded to your computer or to an iPod.

Research

Content on the Internet is variable. As we have already noted, at one level the information can be surprisingly good – scientific papers, articles and books. (Google has already scanned over 10 million books from major American and European libraries, which makes it the largest library in the world.) You can download literary masterpieces through the Gutenberg Project.[18] At a more remote level, content may not be entirely accurate, and may be difficult to trace – there are no borders on the Internet.

When using the Internet as a research resource you should:

- analyse and critically appraise the material available
- check the origin of the source material
- beware of any bias that may be apparent – look out for propaganda
- beware of ethical issues, for example plagiarism
- check for copyright. Copyright restrictions apply on the Internet. Always ask permission when using other people's work or images. It is permissible to reproduce a small part of a work, where it is pertinent[19]
- know how to use search engines effectively.

Commercial, Public Relations and Marketing

The Internet is used to transact business in many areas, for example:

- online banking
- PayPal – which makes it safe and easy for individuals to buy or sell goods on the Internet
- e-mail
- advertising

- online shopping
- digital content, for example journals, newspapers, audio books, MP3 tracks.

The power of the Internet as a resource in the commercial, public relations and marketing fields was evidenced in the American presidential election of 2008, when the Democratic candidate Barack Obama was elected as the 44th President of the United States. His campaign utilised the Internet effectively; supporters collected funds using databases, sent e-mails and reached out to Middle America. They also used Twitter and Facebook to get his message across. His campaign was widely admired for its effectiveness. President Barack Obama has his own website, and he still uses the Internet to deliver weekly addresses from the White House.[20]

It is now apparent that the effective use of modern Internet technologies, exceptional personal communication skills and leadership can all combine together to produce effective results.

As we have seen, the Internet is redefining our world. As to how we manage cyberspace – that is for us and the future to decide.

EXERCISE

Briefly answer the following questions.

- Define the term 'Internet'.
- What does the acronym ARPANET stand for?
- Who is known as the 'father of the Internet'?
- What is the IP protocol responsible for?
- What is the TCP protocol responsible for?
- Define the World Wide Web.
- What is a browser?
- What does the acronym HTTP stand for?
- What does the acronym HTML stand for?
- Name the person who is accredited with the introduction of the World Wide Web.
- CERN announced the World Wide Web would be free to all on what date?
- Who owns the Internet?
- Why was the ISCO established?
- Name two ways of communicating on the Web.
- Is copyright law applicable to the Internet?
- Name some of the factors that are important when using the Internet as a research tool.
- Name two institutions that provide online training.

References and Resources

1   http://www.ibiblio.org/pioneers/licklider.html; http://www.isoc.org/internet/history/brief.shtml; and http://www.velocityguide.com/internet-history/jcr-licklider.html
2   http://www.computerhistory.org/
3   http://cyber.law.harvard.edu/icann/pressingissues2000/briefingbook/dnshistory.html
4   http://www.livinginternet.com/i/ii
5   Ibid.
6   Ibid.
7   Ibid.
8   http://www.livinginternet.com/i/ii_nsfnet.htm
9   http://www.livinginternet.com/i/ii
10 http://info.cern.ch/Proposal.html
11 http://info.cern.ch/
12 http://www.isoc.org/educpillar/resources/docs/promote-ixp-guide.pdf. (attribution: Mike Jensen)
13 http://www.isoc.org/isoc/mission/
14 Charter of the Internet Architecture Board: http://www.ietf.org/rfc/rfc2850.txt
15 http://www.irtf.org/
16 http://www.iana.org/
17 http://www.isoc.org/isoc/fin/sop_2009.pdf
18 http://www.gutenberg.org/
19 David Dolowitz, Steve Buckler and Fionnghuala Sweeney, *Researching Online* (Palgrave Study Skills), Gill & Macmillan (June 2008)
20 http://www.barackobama.com/

② Connecting to the Internet

As we saw in Chapter 1, the Internet is a vast global network of networked computers. To avail of its features we have to establish a connection to this network of networks.

What do You Need to Connect to the Internet?

To connect to the Internet, you will need:

- a computer
- an account with an Internet Service Provider (ISP), which will provide you with an Internet connection. This can be either
  - a dial-up connection, or
  - a Broadband connection
- software designed to allow you to browse the Web and to send and receive e-mail.

Internet Service Providers (ISPs)

The first step in connecting to the Internet is to sign up with an ISP. Most ISPs are telecommunication companies, for example Eircom.

An ISP's primary task is to provide the following services (these may vary from ISP to ISP):

- a connection to the Internet
- the possibility to have multiple e-mail accounts
- hosting services for your website
- online storage and security services.

Types of Connection

Dial-up (Narrowband)

A dial-up connection is the most basic type of connection. It uses the existing land line telephone system. It is slow (relative to broadband) and is intermittent. It is only on when a connection is established – then the telephone receiver is effectively off the hook and your telephone line is engaged. This is a major disadvantage.

A modem is needed to make a dial-up connection. This converts a computer's native digital signal into a signal that can be sent down the telephone line. ('Modem' is short for modulator demodulator.)

Broadband

A broadband connection is characterised by being fast (in comparison to dial-up) and always on. Broadband uses various methods or technologies to connect to the Internet. These include:

- ADSL (Asymmetric Digital Subscriber Line). This uses the existing telephone copper wire which connects your house to the exchange. The distance of your house from your local telephone exchange will determine whether you can use an ADSL connection.
- Cable. Requires a digital TV cable service in your area. This can offer very high speed.
- Wireless technologies that provide service over larger areas, both metropolitan and rural:
  — Wireless – using services provided by cable companies to distribute TV in rural areas. The consumer has a special aerial to receive the signal.
  — Wi-Fi hot spots in airports, hotels and urban areas. This is a short-range system and uses the same Wi-Fi technology that is used in the home.
  — The new government National Broadband Scheme, which will deliver broadband to more sparsely populated rural areas using mobile technology. In even more remote areas the government will subsidise satellite connection.
  — Mobile broadband using 3G technology – available anywhere your mobile phone works.
  — Satellite, which has a large area coverage. The service is relatively slow and there are latency issues. (Latency is the delay that occurs along the transmission path.)

Monthly Cost and Initial Connection Cost

The cost of connecting to the Internet depends on the service provided and on the particular charges applied by individual ISPs for that service. In the Irish market there are a number of companies offering a connection to the Internet. (See www.broadband.ie for a comparison of the various services.)

The main cost for an individual is the fixed monthly charge. There may be an installation charge which typically will include the supply of a router. There are of course many different types of router.

Some ISPs will set a download limit on the maximum number of Mbps (megabits per second) or Gbps (gigabits per second) of data that they will allow you to download per month without additional charge. Remember to check the permitted download as an ISP reserves the right to charge you for any excess data you may have downloaded.

Checklist

Questions to ask before signing up with an ISP:

♦ set-up or connection fee
♦ monthly billing charges
♦ reliability and security of service – check with neighbours
♦ the type of broadband services provided– ADSL, cable, etc.
♦ download and upload speeds
♦ download limit – see above
♦ the contention ratio for your service (the contention ratio is a measure of how many other users are sharing the same telephone line or cable)
♦ additional services – Web hosting and online storage facilities.

Factors that Influence Speed of Access

Bits per Second

Speed on the Internet is measured in bits per second. Bits are the primary '1' and '0' that digital computers work with. In practice we use thousands of bits (kilobits) per second (Kbps) and millions of bits (megabits) per second (Mbps).

The speed of most dial-up connections is 56 Kbps. Broadband speeds are much faster: in Ireland they typically range from 1 Mbps to 10 Mbps. In general, the faster the speed the more expensive the service.

Contention Ratio

The contention ratio is a measure of how many other users are sharing the same telephone line or cable. Again, a high-end service should provide a lower contention ratio. A cheaper service will have a higher contention ratio, and you may notice a decrease in speed around 6.00 p.m. when people arrive home and log on to check their e-mail.

Distance from Exchange (for ADSL Broadband)

Telephone lines impose a limitation on the distance of the subscriber from the telephone exchange. Most households in urban areas can avail of an ADSL service.

Requirements for Connection to the Internet

Most modern computers (PCs or Macs) sold in recent years are perfectly capable of providing a platform to browse the Internet.

The first essential is for the computer to have a piece of hardware that permits a connection to a network. For a laptop computer this will probably be a wireless network card. Desktop computers come with a network card that allows connection to a wired Ethernet LAN.

It is considered advisable to have a firewall, which protects your computer from attack by malicious intruders. It can be a piece of hardware or software. A firewall became part of the XP Operating System Service Pack 2, and Windows 7 has its own very sophisticated firewall.

You will also need: a modem for a dial-up connection or a router, preferably with a firewall, for a broadband connection; a network interface card; a wireless network card (if not already provided); and a filter for an ADSL connection – see below.

Modem and Splitter

A modem converts a computer's native digital signal into a signal that can be sent down the telephone line.

A splitter is a simple device that allows the incoming telephone line to be split into two: one side for the telephone, the other for the modem.

Broadband Connections

For a broadband connection, you need an ADSL router to provide a link between your computer/LAN and the Internet. The router directs the traffic between your computer and the Internet.

Most modern routers come with a wireless access point: this provides Wi-Fi capability. Obviously, depending on the model chosen, routers and their component parts will vary in design, product type and specification.

Network Interface Card (NIC)

This is evidenced by an RJ45 port at the side or rear of the computer (see your computer documentation for more information on how to identify the RJ45 Ethernet port). The task of the NIC card is to convert the computer's internal stream of data into a form that can be transmitted over a network and vice versa.

Wireless Network Card

These are almost universally supplied with laptop computers. Their job is identical to an NIC, except that they use a wireless aerial to transmit and receive data from the wireless access point.

Filter for an ADSL Connection

A filter is needed for an ADSL connection to prevent interference from the ADSL signal on the telephone line. A filter is fitted for each telephone handset.

Software Requirements

- **Connecting to the Internet:** all recent versions of the Windows operating system contain all the components necessary for connecting to the Internet.
- **Connecting to the World Wide Web:** to browse the Web you will need a browser – for example Internet Explorer, Mozilla Firefox.
- **E-mail:** to send and receive conventional Web-based e-mail (as distinct from an e-mail client such as Microsoft Office Outlook 2003, Microsoft Office Outlook 2007 or Windows Live Mail, etc.) you need a Web browser.
- **Specialist software:** other specialist software is available, for example an FTP client, iTunes, and Real Networks.

Setting up Dial-Up and Broadband Internet Connections

Dial-up Connection

When you are setting up an initial connection to the Internet, and are installing software or hardware for the first time, you must follow the guidelines provided by the manufacturer of the hardware/software you are using, and also follow any instructions provided by your ISP. If you run into trouble, contact your ISP's technical support team.

Windows XP

The primary requirements for a dial-up connection with Windows XP are an existing telephone land line and a computer with an internal or an external modem.

We use a standard telephone extension cable (usually supplied) to plug into a telephone socket at one end and into the back of the computer (actually the modem card) at the other end.

If we are using an external modem, we plug the telephone line into that modem, which in turn will be connected to the computer by a USB cable. The hardware has now been installed.

We now need to set up the connection. A connection can be set up as follows:

- Your ISP may have supplied you with a CD to help you through the set-up process on the computer – insert the CD and follow the instructions.
- Or use the Windows XP 'New Connection Wizard' as follows:

- — Click Start > All Programs > Accessories > Communications > New Connection Wizard. Select 'Connect to the Internet', then 'Set up my Internet connection manually', and 'Connect using a dial-up modem'.
- — On the following screens, you'll be asked to type in information provided by your ISP: the local phone number that connects your PC to your ISP, your user name and your password.

Windows Vista or Windows 7

To set up a dial-up connection using either the Windows Vista or the Windows 7 operating systems:

- Click on 'Start', and then select the Control Panel.
- Click on 'Network and Sharing Center'.
- Then click on the 'Set Up a Connection or Network' link (Vista) or 'Set Up a New Connection or Network' link (Windows 7).
- Choose a connection option – 'Set up a dial-up connection' – then click Next.
- Enter the information provided by your ISP: the local phone number that connects your PC to your ISP, your user name and your password.
- Click Connect.

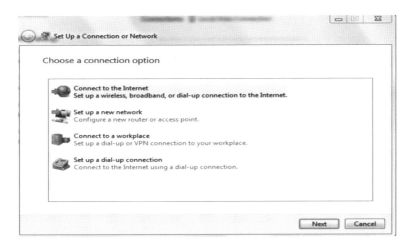

Broadband Connection

ADSL Broadband using Vista or Windows 7

The steps involved in setting up an ADSL broadband connection can vary considerably. These factors, among others, will depend on the services offered by your ISP.

To set up a connection using Windows Vista and Windows 7 you will need to have the following:

- an old-fashioned telephone land line
- your user name and password, which you will have received from your ISP
- your router, which should have already been correctly configured and connected to your computer. A connection may be made by connecting a USB cable, an Ethernet cable or wirelessly.

To connect to the Internet:

- Click on Control Panel and then on the Network and Sharing Center icon.
- Then click on 'Set up a Connection or Network' link (Vista) or 'Set up a New Connection or Network' link (Windows 7).
- A new window will open – 'Choose a Network Connection'.
- Select 'Connect to the Internet – Set up a wireless, broadband, or dial-up connection to the Internet' (see above). Click Next.
- A new 'How do you want to Connect' window will now open: select PPPoE.
- A new window opens, 'Connect to the Internet'.
- Enter your user name and password in the appropriate fields and click Connect.

Setting up a Cable Connection

Cable connections require a digital TV cable service in your area. The process of installing a cable connection is very similar to the ADSL connection.

Setting up a Fixed Wireless Connection

A fixed wireless broadband connection requires an aerial attached either to your roof or to an external wall.

Setting up a Satellite Connection

Your ISP will provide a satellite dish and the ancillary equipment. There are, however, latency issues. In some rural areas, this may be the only form of broadband internet connection service available.

IP Addresses and Domain Names

IP Addresses

To access the Internet, every connection needs a unique address – an IP (Internet Protocol) address. This address is assigned automatically by your ISP each time a connection is made to the Internet. In the case of *broadband,* an always-on connection, the address does not change unless the router is switched off or there is a power outage. Should this occur, your ISP will automatically assign a new IP address to your connection.

We say 'connection' rather than 'computer' because if there is more than one computer on a LAN (local area network), each computer shares the same external IP address. Each individual computer within the LAN is assigned an internal IP address by the router. As an analogy, think of a hotel: it will have a street address, its external address; but each guest will have a room number, the internal address.

This internal addressing adds a level of security to individual computers because they are hidden behind the external face of the router, which is the only device directly connected to the outside network – the Internet. Technically this is called Network Address Translation (NAT).

An IP address is 32 bits long, and this is converted into decimal format, for example 89.207.56.140: this is the decimal representation of the binary code. This is easier to handle than 32 bits of binary '1' and '0'. But a name, e.g. www.rte.ie, is much easier. This is where the domain name comes in.

Domain Names

The domain name system is fundamental to the operation of the Internet. It takes the 32-bit IP address and translates it into a name that we can recognise. Take www.rte.ie: www.rte.ie is the domain name; rte is the sub-domain; and .ie is the upper domain. We are all familiar with the top-level domains .com, .ie, .org, etc.

A personal domain name is your own unique address on the Internet. Your Internet address, assuming you wish to have your upper domain or suffix as .ie, would be www.yourname.ie. You could of course also choose another domain, such as .eu or .com, etc.

The .ie Domain Registry (www.domainregistry.ie) maintains a registry of all .ie registered Internet names. You can check there to find out if your name is still available for use.

Requirements

You will be asked to complete an application form when you register a Domain Name. If you are based in Ireland, you are required to supply the relevant documentation. Information on this is available at www.domainregistry.ie/faq.php#1. In most cases, your ISP will arrange registration for you and provide you with a Web hosting service. A list of authorised resellers for the .ie domain is available at www.domainregistry.ie.

E-Mail Client Program

To send an e-mail, as opposed to Web e-mail, you need an e-mail client program installed on your computer, e.g. Microsoft Office Outlook 2003, Microsoft Office Outlook 2007, Windows Live Mail, etc. You have to configure your client program. For this you will need:

- your name
- a password
- your e-mail address (e.g. myname@eircom.net), which will have already been agreed with your ISP.

It may also be necessary to know the protocol for your incoming mail server, e.g. POP3, and outgoing mail server, e.g. SMTP or IMAP.

Adding a New E-mail Account

Microsoft Office Outlook 2003

- Click Start > All Programs > Microsoft Office > Microsoft Office Outlook 2003. Microsoft Office Outlook 2003 will now open.
- Select the Tools menu and click on the 'E-mail accounts' command.
- The E-mail Account Wizard window will now open. Select the radio button next to 'Add a new e-mail account'. Click Next.
- The 'Server Type' window now opens. Select the option you need – usually POP3 – and click Next.
- The 'Internet E-mail Settings (POP3)' window now opens. Fill in the information:
  - user information – your name and your e-mail address, e.g. username@eircom.net; then click check box adjacent to 'Remember password'
  - logon information – username and password
  - server information – enter type (e.g. mail1.eircom.net) into both the Incoming Mail server (POP3) and Outgoing Mail server (SMTP).
- Click the 'Test Account Settings' button (requires network connection). Click Next. The 'Congratulations' window now opens.
- Click Finish.

Microsoft Office Outlook 2007

- Click Start > All Programs > Microsoft Office > Microsoft Office Outlook 2007. Microsoft Office Outlook 2007 will open.
- Select the Tools menu and click on the 'Accounts Settings' command. The 'Accounts Settings' window will open.
- Select the New icon.

- The 'Choose an e-mail service' window will now open and the default settings Microsoft Exchange, POP3, IMAP or HTTP will already have been selected. Click Next.
- The 'Auto Account Setup' window will open.
- Fill in the requested information – your name, e-mail address and password – and retype your password. The password is the password your ISP has given you.
- Click the check box next to 'Manually configure server settings or additional server types'. Click Next.
- A new window now opens: 'Choose an E-Mail Service'. Select the 'Internet and E-Mail' radio button, then click Next.
- The 'Internet and E-Mail Settings' window will now open. Fill in the requested information:

— user information – enter your name and your e-mail address, e.g. username@eircom.net
— server information – select account type (usually POP3); then enter incoming and outgoing server type (e.g. mail1.eircom.net) into both the incoming mail server (POP3) and outgoing mail server (SMTP)
— logon information – username and password.
- Click check box next to 'Remember password'.
- Click the 'Test Account Settings' button. (Requires network connection.) Click Next. The 'Congratulations' window now opens.
- Click Finish.

EXERCISE

Answer the following questions.
- What do you need to connect to the Internet?
- What does the acronym ISP stand for?
- What is the primary task of an ISP?
- Name two different ways of connecting to the Internet.
- Explain the term 'contention ratio'.
- What is a router?
- Why do you need a firewall?
- What is an IP address?
- Check the following website: www.domainregistry.ie/faq.php#1. Write a brief note on the documentation required to obtain a personal domain name.
- Give an example of a domain name.

---

3 World Wide Web and Search Engines

Introduction

What is the World Wide Web?

The World Wide Web is part of the Internet. Specifically, the Web is a collection of web pages.

What is a Browser?

A browser is an application that allows you to do the following:

- Access Web resources using the Hypertext Transfer Protocol (HTTP). (HTTP is a set of rules, i.e. a protocol.) It interprets HyperText Mark-up Language (HTML) and downloads web pages, which can include text, graphics, audio content and moving images. This data is then presented in the form of a page on your computer screen. This page will include the graphic images, possibly audio and very often nowadays a moving 'flash' video advertisement.
- Navigate easily from one page to another by clicking on hyperlinks.

In this chapter we shall be using Internet Explorer as our Web browser. Other Web browsers include Mozilla Firefox, Google Chrome and (for Mac users) Apple Safari.

Browsing with Internet Explorer

To open Windows Internet Explorer, either click on the Start menu and then select the Internet Explorer icon, or click on the icon on your desktop.

If you are connecting to the Internet via a dial-up connection, you will need to dial up your ISP. You then enter your user name and password, and then click the Connect button.

Internet Explorer will take you to a start page, which is your home page. Set your home page as follows:

- Go to the Tools menu.
- Click on the 'Internet Options' command. The Internet Options dialogue box will now open.
- Click the General tab.
- Enter the website address in the list box.
- Click Apply and OK.

- The *address bar* is the bar below the title bar. It displays the address of the current web page. You can enter a Web address into the address bar. A web address is known as a Universal Resource Locator (URL).
- The *back and forward buttons* record the order in which the web pages have been visited. The back button will bring you back to a previously visited web page and the forward button reverses the process. You can also use the down arrow, to the right of the forward button, to select a specific web page to return to.

- Click the *refresh* button to reload the current page you are visiting.

- Click the *stop* button if you want to stop a web page downloading.

- A *link* in a website is usually displayed in a different font or colour and may be underlined. The link may take you to a different section within the current page, or to a new website or page. When you click on a link, the mouse pointer may change to a hand motif.

EXERCISE 1

- Open the Visit Dublin Webcam page: http://www.visitdublin.com/multimedia/DublinWebcam/dublin.aspx
- Click the 'Stop' button. Then, to refresh the page, click the 'Refresh' button.
- Click on a new link, 'Podcasts'.
- Click on 'Check out our full iWalks Series!'
- Select the 'Temple Bar to Dockland' walk.
- Click Download Brochure. A new download window will now open: 'pdf/iWalk5_Temple_Bar_to_the_Docklands.pdf'.
- View Web page.
- Close .pdf file.
- Click the 'Home' button to return to the 'Home' page.
- Close Internet Explorer 7.

Tabs

Internet Explorer 7 and Internet Explorer 8 incorporate tabs, which allow us to open different web pages in the one browser window.

Accessing tabs:

- Open the website http://www.rte.ie

- New Tab icon:

- To open the 'Television' web page in a new tab, press the Ctrl key and then click on the 'Television' link. To switch from one tabbed web page to another, click on the Tab List arrow. The window below shows tabs accessed in Internet Explorer 7.

Quick Tab button   To close tab, click x

Click this arrow to view websites you entered in the address field

To switch between visited websites, click the down arrow

- To open a new tab, click on the 'New Tab' button.

- This will open a new web page in the browser window.
- Then enter the new URL in the address field.

Tab Options

- To set the tab options, go to the Tools menu.
- Then select the 'Internet Options' command.
- Click the General tab.

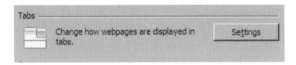

- Under the 'Tabs' section, click 'Settings'.
- Click OK.
- A new Tabbed Browsing Settings dialogue box will now open.
- Click the check boxes or radio buttons to set your preferred options.
- Click OK.

Links

An explanation of the various types of links in web pages is given in the Web Authoring section of this book.

To navigate from link to link in a web page, right click on the link and select 'Open in New Tab'.

Links Bar

The links bar is used to store the addresses of the websites you visit most often. For example, you might have links to the three Irish broadsheets, or to RTÉ, Met Éireann and your bank.

To create a link, drag the Address icon from the Address bar and drop it on the Links bar.

To navigate from a link within the Links bar, right click on Link and select 'Open'.

Accessing User Elements in Internet Explorer 7

Page Source

You can access a page source as follows:

- Right click on the web page. A context-sensitive menu now opens. Select the 'View Source' command.

- The Notepad window will now open. The data notepad page shows the source code behind the web page. Elements shown can include the author of the document, the address of the website and the date when the site was last updated.

```
player[1] - Notepad                                    _ □ ×
File  Edit  Format  View  Help

<!DOCTYPE html PUBLIC "-//W3C//DTD XHTML 1.0 Transitional//EN" "http://w
<html xmlns="http://www.w3.org/1999/xhtml">

<head>
<title>RTÉ Radio: Gadgets</title>
<script src="silverlight.js" type="text/javascript"></script>
<link href="/grids/css/rte_global_03.css" rel="stylesheet" type="text/css" />
<!--[if lte IE 6]>
<link href="/grids/css/ie6.css" rel="stylesheet" type="text/css" />
```

Page Properties

- To view the Page Properties, right click on the web page. A new menu will now open.
- Select the 'Properties' command.
- The Properties dialogue box opens. View document properties.

Page Information

To view 'Page Information', right click on the web page, and then select the 'Page Info' command.

Favorites

When you find a website or web page of particular interest, its URL can be saved as a 'Favorite' (Internet Explorer) or Bookmark (Mozilla Firefox).

Using the Favorites Menu

Make sure the web page whose address you want to save in 'Favorites' is displayed in your browser.
- Click on the Favorites menu.
- Select the 'Add to Favorites' command.

- The Add to Favorites dialogue box now opens. The name of the website automatically appears in the 'Name' field. You can shorten the name by editing it.

- Click 'Add' to add the address to your list of 'Favorites'.
- Or, if you want to save a Web address in a subject folder:

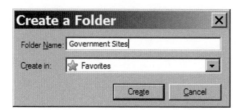

- — click on the 'New Folder' button, and enter the name of the new folder in 'Folder Name' field. A 'Create a Folder' window now opens.
- — enter the folder name as, e.g. Government Sites, and click Create. You can now save all your government websites in your new folder.

To open a 'Favorite' (a website address you have already saved):

- Click on Favorites menu, and select the website you want to go to.
- Then right click on 'Favorite/link' and select 'Open'.
- Should you wish to cut, copy, or delete a 'Favorite' listed in your 'Favorites' centre, click on the Favorites menu, select folder or link, and then choose the option you want.

Organising favourites:

- Click on the Favorites menu and select the 'Organize Favorites' command.

- The Organize Favorites dialogue box will now open. Click on the item you wish to organise.
- Click the New Folder, Move, Rename or Delete button.
- Then click Close.

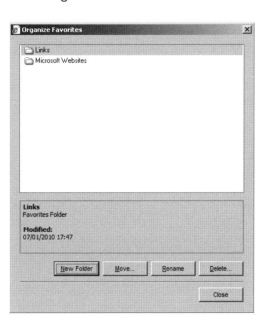

RSS Feeds

RSS stands for Really Simple Syndication or Rich Site Summary. It is used to update frequently accessed digital content such as news and podcasts. If a website contains an RSS feed, the RSS icon will be displayed as follows:

SUBSCRIBE TO WORLD UPDATES

Click on the 'Subscribe' link, which will be displayed in the web page. A new window may open: select your 'Reader'.

You can view your Feeds in the 'Favorites Center' with Internet Explorer as follows:

- Click the Favorites Center icon, then select the Feeds tab, and select feed.

- Click on the Feeds icon and select the feed you want. A brief headline will appear. If you want to view the entire content of the feed, click on the 'View Online' link. Your feed will then open in Windows Internet Explorer 7.

If you want to delete, copy or move a feed, click on the Feeds tab in the Favorites Center, select your feed, right click and then select your option from the menu which now appears.

Setting Feed Properties

You can set the number of updates you wish to save for a feed and how often you wish to receive feeds through the Feed Properties dialogue box as follows:

- Open Windows Internet Explorer.
- Go to the Favorites Center.
- Click on the Feeds icon.
- Right click on 'Feed', select 'Properties' from the menu which will have opened, then select options in the Feed Properties dialogue box.
- Click OK.

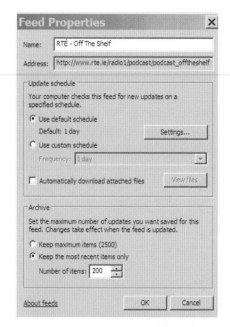

To change the default feed update schedule:

- Click the Settings tab in the Feed Properties dialogue box. The Feed Settings dialogue box will open.
- Click in the check boxes to select options.
- Click OK.

History

Should you wish to view a list of the websites you have visited over a period of weeks or days, you can do so through the 'History' section in the Favorites Center in Internet Explorer.

To access the History tab:

- Open your browser.
- Click on the Favorites Center icon.
- Select the History tab.
- Click the down arrow to the right of the History tab to select your viewing mode.
- Select the day or week you are interested in viewing.
- You can click on the link to open a website you want to visit.

To delete your browsing history:

- Click on the Tools menu and select the 'Internet Options' command. A new Internet Options dialogue box now opens.
- Click on the General tab.
- Move to the Browsing History section and then click on the Delete tab. The Delete Browsing History dialogue box will now open.
- Click on the Delete History tab.

- Click OK.

If you want to specify how long Internet Explorer should keep a record of the websites you have visited:

- Click on the 'Settings' button, which is to the right of the 'Delete' button, in the Internet Options dialogue box.
- A new dialogue box opens – Temporary Internet Files and History.

Temporary Internet Files and His... ×

- Move to 'Days to keep pages in history'. Click arrow and select your preferred number of days.
- Click OK.

History
Specify how many days Internet Explorer should save the list of websites you have visited.

Days to keep pages in history: 20

OK   Cancel

Find Text on Page

To find text on a page:

- Select the Edit menu.
- Click the 'Find on Page' command.
- Enter the text you are searching for in the 'Find' field.

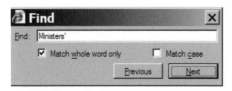

- Click Next.
- Click X to close the Find toolbar.

Windows Internet Explorer 8 – New Features

In March 2009 Microsoft updated their Windows Internet Explorer 7 with Windows Internet Explorer 8. The following pages will identify most of the newer features which were not available in Internet Explorer 7.

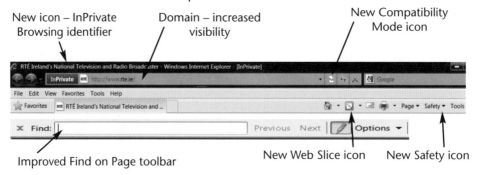

New security elements include:

- InPrivate Browsing
- InPrivate Filtering
- SmartScreen Filter.

These features are accessible through the Safety menu which is available on the Command bar or on the Menu bar through the Tools menu.

InPrivate Browsing

InPrivate Browsing allows you to browse the Web without Internet Explorer storing data such as cookies, history, etc. This is important if you are using shared computers because of the security implications.

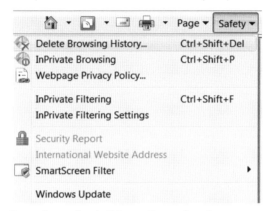

To activate the InPrivate Browsing feature:

- Open your browser.
- Select the 'InPrivate Browsing' command either from the Safety menu on the Command bar or from the Tools menu on the Menu bar.
- The InPrivate identifier will then appear in your address bar.

InPrivate Filtering

InPrivate Filtering was designed to allow you to have a measure of control over the content level and choice of information a third party website may have access to.

To enable InPrivate Filtering:

- Open your browser.
- Select the InPrivate Filtering feature command either from the Safety menu on the Command bar or from the Tools menu on the Menu bar.
- To customise your settings:
  — click on the 'InPrivate Setting' command
  — select the appropriate option
  — click OK.

SmartScreen Filter

The SmartScreen Filter offers further security measures: for example, this feature can help track and block malicious websites. You also have the options of checking out a website you are visiting and reporting an unsafe website (see overleaf).

To enable the SmartScreen Filter:

- Select the Safety icon on the Command bar.
- Select and click on the 'SmartScreen Filter' command from the menu.
- The submenu will now open. Click on the 'Turn on SmartScreen Filter' command.

Compatibility Viewing Mode

Compatibility Viewing Mode enables you to view websites designed for earlier browsers, for example IE6 or IE7.

To activate compatibility viewing, click on the Compatibility icon to the left of the Refresh icon on the address bar.

Compatibility settings are set in the Compatibility View Settings dialogue box. This is opened by activating the 'Compatibility View Settings' command on the Tools menu.

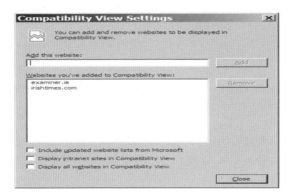

Accelerators

Accelerators allow you to use a search engine, translate a page and directly map any address, etc. from your existing web page.

- Highlight the appropriate text in the web page.
- Click on the Accelerator icon.

- You will now have access to the submenu. Select the appropriate command, for example Map with Live Search (see opposite).

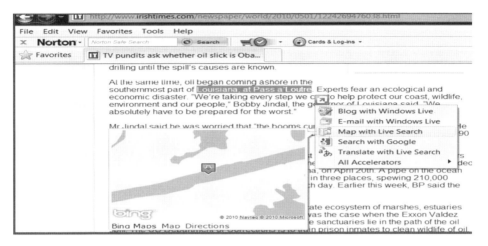

Web Slices

Web slices allow you to check for updated content from a specific website/web page, for example the latest news from Reuters, directly from your Favorites bar.

- First, note that a Web Slice icon will only appear on the Command bar when the website/web page you are visiting supports web slices.
- To view and subscribe to web slices you will need to click on the Web Slice icon
- Then select the web slice you wish to subscribe to.

- A new window now opens which enables you to add the web slice to your Favorites bar.
- Click on the 'Add to Favorites' button.

When an update is available the web slice will be highlighted on your Favorites bar.

Improved Find on Page Toolbar

To activate the Find on Page toolbar, select the 'Find on Page' command from the Edit menu. The Find on Page toolbar searches for matches to the text while you are entering the text in the field box.

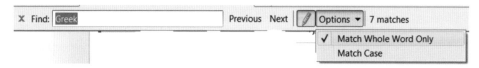

To close the Find on Page toolbar, click the Close icon.

Anatomy of a URL Address

Each website has its own unique Web address, referred to as a Uniform Resource Locator.
The following fictitious Web address consists of the elements listed below:
http://www.canalbookshop.ie/european/historical_reports.htm

- http://   Hypertext Transfer Protocol – a protocol used to access the Web
- www.canalbookshop.ie   the name of the website
- www   the www is the host – the web pages are on the World Wide Web
- canalbookshop   the second-level domain name
- .ie   the top or upper-level domain name
- european   the name of the folder in which the file 'historical reports' is stored
- historical_reports   the name of the file stored in the European folder
- .htm   the file format – HyperText Markup Language is a coding language used to create documents that are intended for viewing in a Web browser.

The following list shows some of the common top-level domain organisational codes:

- .com   commercial organisations (e.g. www.businessopportunitiesireland.com)
- .edu   universities (e.g. www.yale.edu)
- .gov   government agencies
- .net   networks
- .org   usually applies to a non-profit-making organisation.

Internet codes for countries contain two letters. For example:

- .ie   Ireland (e.g. www.ucd.ie)
- .fr   France (e.g. www.louvre.fr)
- .de   Germany
- .hk   Hong Kong
- .dk   Denmark

A number of countries show both the organisational code and the country code in the top-level domain. In fact they use two suffixes, for example www.yahoo.co.uk

Useful website: http://www.iana.org/domains/root/db/

For information on acquiring an .ie domain name visit http://www.domainregistry.ie/faq.php

EXERCISES

1 Find the top-level domain codes for the following:
   - a museum
   - an international organisation
   - a military site.

2 What is the Internet country code for the following countries?
   - Italy
   - Poland
   - Spain

Search Engines

The Internet has opened up a whole world of possibilities in which vast amounts of data can be accessed by anyone with a computer and a connection to the Internet.

Originally, the Internet was developed as a means of effectively exchanging research and information between establishments, most of which were universities. Initially this led to the development of e-mail for direct communication and to the use of the newly developed file transfer mechanism (FTP) for transferring computer files over telephone lines. It also led to discussion groups using the Usenet.

Then in 1991 the World Wide Web was developed with a graphical user interface and hypertext point and click navigation. This mix of a visual interface and an easy means of navigation started the rapid growth of the Information Age.

There is a huge archive of written material which forms part of the vast store of information in the world today. Newspapers are digitising their archives, and Google has a project to digitise all books.

In this section we shall look at the tools we use to search for information on the World Wide Web, specifically search engines, and human edited directories or catalogues. We shall consider when to use specific search engines for research and some of the various search options that are available.

How do Search Engines Work?

A search engine searches for information which has been entered into a search field. Different types of search engine work in different ways. Search engines retrieve information and then display this information on their web pages.

Types of Search Engine

Crawlers

These search engines use spiders, or robots (programs) to crawl through websites, building lists of words, noting the links to other pages and corresponding websites. Crawlers are good for finding specific information.

Example: Google (http://www.google.com).

Internet Directories or Catalogues

Internet catalogues/directories are created by humans and then divided into categories. Catalogues only list websites. The topics are organised in a hierarchical structure. For example, a top-level heading might be 'Arts'. Click on this and you are led to the next level, 'Humanities', and then you can select 'History', etc. There may be more layers in the hierarchy before you come to the links to specific websites. You navigate downwards through directory levels by clicking on the appropriate links.

Internet directories are good for finding topics, and conventional wisdom suggests that the quality of the retrieved data is superior to that from a normal search.

Example: Open Directory Project (http://www.dmoz.org/).

Metacrawler Search Engines

Metacrawler search engines do not have their own database. Instead they transmit a search to other search engines simultaneously and then list the results in their own web page.

They are good as a comparison of what is available on other search engines.

Example – Dogpile (http://www.dogpile.com).

Most Visited Search Engines

There are hundreds of search engines. Among the most visited are:

- Google (crawler) – http://www.google.com. The Google database contains over 8 billion web pages. (Source: http://www.google.ie/intl/en/options/)
- Google Scholar – http://www.scholar.google.com). Good for research: listings contain articles, reprints, library links, etc.
- Yahoo! (crawler) – http://www.yahoo.com
- Bing (crawler) – http://www.bing.com. Microsoft's most recent search engine.
- Dogpile (metacrawler) – htpp://www.dogpile.com
- Open Project Directory (directory/catalogue) – http://www.dmoz.org

For a more academic search visit Intute at http://www.intute.ac.uk.

Both Google (http://www.directory.google.com) and Yahoo! (dir.yahoo.com) have their own directory. Google accesses the Open Project Directory listings.

If you want to ask a direct question, consider searching answers.com (http//:www.answers.com).

To compare search engine features, visit http://www.searchengineshowdown.com/features/byfeature.shtml

Searching (Crawler)

To carry out a search, open your browser window. You can then either:

- Enter your query (i.e. the key words you will use for your search) in the 'Instant Search' box to the right of the address field, then click on the Search icon.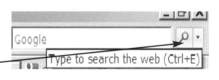
- To select a different search provider, click on the down arrow.

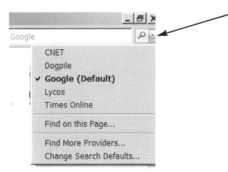

- Or you can enter the search engine's URL in the address field. Then press 'Enter'.

- Enter your keywords in the 'Search' field and then click the 'Search' button.

- Google's main website home page is shown above.
- There are links to various topics: Images, News, etc. The search aid links to 'Images', etc. are at the top of the page above the Search box. Further options are displayed in the left-hand column under 'Web'.
- Hyperlinks to web pages are displayed in the centre, and to the right are some sponsored links. Retrieval results number 8,540,000.

Refining your Search

You can refine your results by entering Boolean operators. You enter a query in the search field and then use the operators to find a solution. The following examples show how the operators work.

- Use + and – symbols to include or exclude words. No spaces after + or – signs, so, for example: james joyce +author.
- 'and' requires that *both* terms are returned (French and Italian bread).

- 'or' will return *either* result (Irish or American jazz).

- To search for an exact word order use double quotation marks, e.g. "Chestnut Trees in Ireland". Using quotation marks reduces the number of pages found and makes searching easier.

- If you are not sure of the exact word or phrase, or if the results would be different if you used American or English spelling, consider using the 'wild card' symbol *, e.g. 'colo*r' will find color and colour.

Advanced Search Page

Click the 'Advanced' search link if you wish to limit your results to a specific file format (e.g. PDF, Word, PowerPoint, Rich Text) or domain name or date range, etc. Enter your query, keyword or phrase in the appropriate field, click the down arrow and then select the option from the list that appears. Finally, click the 'Advanced Search' button.

Web Directories or Catalogues

To search topics in the Open Project Directory (http://www.dmoz.org/) you must work your way through the directory levels.

- Open Directory – Home Page – Categories/General Subjects – Top Level.
- Click on the 'Computer' hyperlink to move through the hierarchical levels.

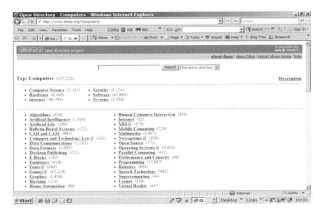

- The sub-directory is now shown under 'Computers'. Note that the number of websites for each topic is shown in parentheses. We are moving down through the hierarchical levels, from a broad base to a narrower base.

Metacrawler Search

Metacrawler search engines are good for reviewing and contrasting results that are available on other search engines. For example, the search engines accessed by Dogpile are Google, Yahoo! and Live Search. (Be aware of the sponsored links.) Note that you can further refine your search by clicking on the links under 'Are you looking for?' on the right-hand side of the results page. (Dogpile is at http//:www.dogpile.com.)

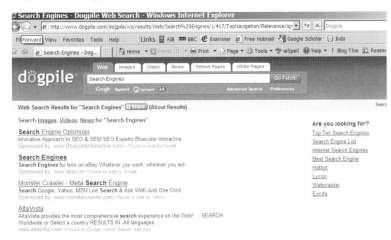

Summary

- When searching, think about the keywords you are going to use in your search.
- Know when to use a specific search engine, e.g. Google or Google Scholar for articles, etc. Use metacrawler engines for an overall view.

- Where the search engine permits, use Boolean operators.
- Use Internet directories for researching topics.
- Always analyse your results and be aware of content. Check the source and URL, and the upper domain.
- Use encyclopaedias such as http//:www.wikipedia.org – again, check sources.

EXERCISE

- Carry out the searches mentioned in the illustrations in this chapter, using the various search engines referred to.
- Which search engine do you prefer to use?
- List the various types of search engine.
- What are Boolean operators and why are they used?

Downloading Files

Modern digital computers store their data in computer files. A file is the container in which the digital information, e.g. a letter, a photograph or a song, is stored. Files can be stored on hard disks, floppy disks, flash drives, CD, DVD and magnetic tape.

In the Microsoft Windows environment different file types are distinguished by their letter file extension, for example .doc or .docx (Word 2007 XML document). The .doc or .docx is the file extension, which tells Windows, through its file association rule, that this is registered as a Word file.

To view the file extensions for file types, open the following paths:

- In Windows Explorer XP go to: Menu > Tools > Folder Options > File Types.
- In Windows Vista or Windows 7 go to: Control Panel > Default Programs. Click on the link 'Associate a file type or protocol with a specific program'. A new 'Set Associations' window will now open. Select the appropriate option and click Close.

In Windows, files are grouped or organised into folders, just as you would put a paper document into a cardboard or plastic folder and then into a filing cabinet. This arrangement allows you to organise and locate files on a hard disk. Files can be bundled and compressed into a special type of folder: the files are then said to be zipped and the folder is called a zip folder.

Files are loaded – i.e. moved or transferred – on to a computer in different ways. When you buy a new program you typically receive it on a CD. You run the CD by putting it into the CD drive and thereby start the process of transferring the files to your computer's hard disk.

Alternatively you can download files from the Web or attach them to an e-mail and send them to whomsoever.

When you decide to download files from the Internet to your computer, you are transferring a copy of the file from the Internet to your computer.

Real Audio and Video File Formats

These are proprietary audio and video formats developed by Real Networks and are supported by the RealPlayer media player. Real Networks also support streaming audio and video. Many broadcasting organisations 'stream' programme content to the Web using Real Networks audio and video. Streaming is the process whereby you listen to or watch the content almost instantaneously as it is downloaded/received.

You can download digital media players from the Internet, e.g. iTunes, RealPlayer or Windows Media Player. We shall now look at downloading the Windows Media Player 11, which allows you to play media files.

To Download Windows Media Player 11

- Open your browser.
- Enter the URL for Microsoft: http://www.microsoft.com/windows/windowsmedia/player/11/default.aspx
- Click on the 'Download Now' hyperlink.
- There is the possibility that a file you download from the Internet could contain a virus, so be cautious. Security Warning Boxes will appear. Be sure that you only 'Run' or 'Save' executable files that come from a site you trust.

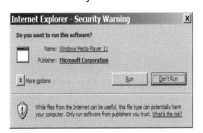

- When you have clicked the appropriate option, a new dialogue box now opens showing the file name and extension (.exe), the progress and transfer rate.

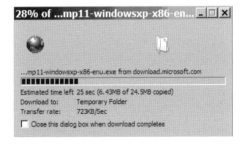

- As the Windows Media Player is part of Windows, you will be asked to validate your copy of Windows in the validation window.

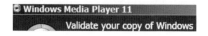

- Click on the' Validate' link.

- A new window opens indicating the final installation progress.

To view file types linked to Windows Media Player in XP:

- Open the Windows Media Player application.
- Click on the Tools menu.
- Select the 'Options' command from the menu.
- The Options dialogue box will then open. Select the 'File Types' tab.
- Click the check boxes for the default file types required for your media player.
- Click OK.

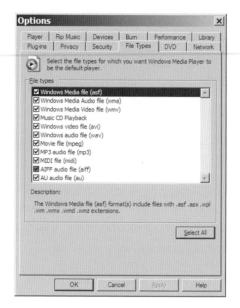

Downloading a Podcast or Video File from Web Pages

As we have seen, programmes can be downloaded directly from the Web. You can download a video or podcast by clicking on the 'Download' link.

To Save a Podcast or Video File

- Open your browser and enter the following URL for RTÉ Radio: http://www.rte.ie/radio/.
- Select 'Podcast' under Downloads/Podcasts.

- Click on the podcast you wish to save.

5 - **Marian Finucane**
RTÉ Radio 1

- A new window will now open. Right click on the podcast link.

- Select 'Save Target As' from the drop-down menu (Windows XP) or 'Save' in the File Download dialogue box (Windows Vista and Windows 7).

Save Target As...

- The Save As dialogue box now opens. Click into the 'Save In' list field and select the destination folder.

Save As
Save in: 🗀 My Podcasts

- You can either accept the file name or change it to another name.

| File name: | Marian Finucane Show ll July 2009 | ▼ | Save |
| Save as type: | MP3 Format Sound | ▼ | Cancel |

- To change the file name, click into the File Name field list and enter the new name.
- 'Save as Type' will be shown as Mp3 Format Sound.
- Click Save.
- The 'Progress' window now opens. When the file has been downloaded a new 'Download complete' window will open.

- Select either the 'Open' button or the 'Close' button.

EXERCISE

- Use the procedures described above to save a podcast of your choice from the RTÉ Radio website.
- Save the file as an Mp3 file.

Downloading a Video File

This section describes how to download a video file from the iTunes U portal at Trinity College Dublin.

First, you must have the iTunes Digital Media Player installed on your computer. This application is free. You can subscribe to iTunes and download the digital media player from the Apple site at http://www.apple.com/itunes/download/

- Enter the following URL in your browser: http:// www.itunes.tcd.ie
- Click on the hyperlink 'Open TCD on iTunes U'.
- You will now be connected to the iTunes U Portal.

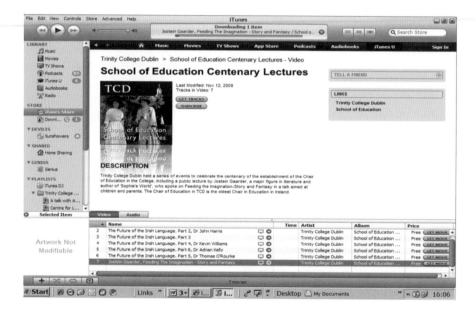

- Select a lecture series you wish to view – see above.
- Click on the Video tab, select a track from the lecture series and then click 'Get Movie'.
- The track will now be downloaded to your hard disk.
- To play the movie, select the listed item from the playlist.

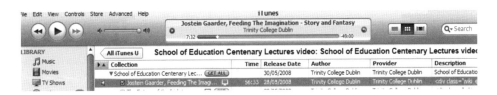

Downloading and Saving Images from Web Pages

First, always be aware of copyright, which applies to all digital media; and remember to reference and attribute your source material.

Download, and save an image from a web page as follows:

- Open your browser.
- Enter the following Web address: http://www.wpclipart.com/holiday/fireworks_1. png.html
- Select an image, for example 'fireworks_l.png'.
- Select option to 'convert to ½.jpg'.
- Right click on the image, then select the 'Save Picture As' command from the context-sensitive menu that now appears.
- The Save Picture dialogue box now opens. Select the destination folder for your graphic.
- Note: the file name is shown as fireworks_1.jpg and the 'save as type' (format) as .JPEG (*.jpg).

- Click 'Save'.

Copying and Pasting Text from a Web Page into a Notepad Document

- Open your browser.
- Enter the Web address for Trinity College Dublin: http://www.tcd.ie
- Select the text you wish to copy.
- Select 'Copy' command in the Edit menu.

- Open Notepad.
- Click on the insertion point
- Go to the Edit menu, select the 'Paste' command and click to insert text
- Save file as 'tcd.txt'.

Saving Web Pages

- Open your browser.
- Enter the Web address for Trinity College Dublin: http://www.tcd.ie
- Select 'Save as' in the File menu.
- The Save Webpage dialogue box will now open.

- Select the destination folder ('Save in' list box).
- Accept or change the file name in the 'File name' list box.
- Click the down arrow to select file format in the 'Save as type' list box.

Save as Type formats:

- *Webpage, complete* (*htm; *html) saves all the files necessary to display the page in their original format. The web page is saved as a separate file and a folder is created to store the graphics, etc.
- *Web Archive, single file* (*mht) saves all the information, including graphics, as a single file.
- *Webpage, HTML only* (*htm; *html) only saves the text on the page but not the graphics or other files. If the web pages contain frames, it will not save each frame. (Frames are separate areas in a web page that act in a similar way to a single page.)
- *Text File* (*.txt) saves the text as plain text without any formatting.

EXERCISE

- Open the website www.tcd.ie
- Save the Trinity College home page (TCD Home) in a Web Archive format.
- Change the file name to TCD.

Printing

Remember, web pages are designed to be viewed on the Web. To facilitate printing a web page, some websites may contain a Print icon. If this is applicable, just click on the icon to print the web page. If no Print icon is available, after previewing the page (see below), click on the File menu and choose Print. The Print dialogue box opens. Check your settings and click Print.

Preview your web page before printing by selecting the 'Print Preview' command from the File menu.

Print Preview

These options may be available on your Print Preview toolbar:

- Click this button to print a web page. This icon button activates the Print dialogue box.

- If you want to change the orientation of the printed web page from the default portrait (vertical) to landscape (horizontal), select the appropriate icon.

- Click this button to activate the Page Setup dialogue box.

- Page Setup can also be accessed through the File menu. Page Setup allows you to:
  — change paper size:

  — select your paper source.

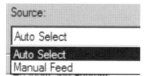

Default Text Coding in Headers and Footers

The heading text coding reads as follows:

Headers and Footers
Header

&w&hPage &p of &P

Explanation	Code
Window Title shown as displayed in the Title Bar	&w
Right aligned text follows &b	&b
Current page number out of total number of pages	&p of &p

The text coding in the footer reads as follows:

Footer

&u&b&d

Explanation	Code
Web page address [URL]	&u
Right aligned text follows &b	&b
Date in short format	&d

Orientation: Click the radio button to change the page orientation.

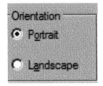

To change the page margins, click into the appropriate list box, enter the new values and click OK.

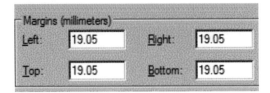

- Select 'Printer' to activate the dialogue box.
- Click list down arrow to change printer. Then click OK.

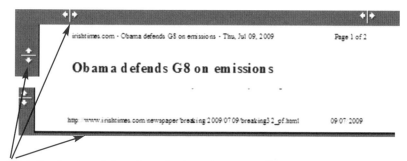

Click the horizontal and vertical markers to adjust page margins.

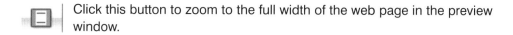 Click this button to zoom to the full width of the web page in the preview window.

 Click this button to view the entire web page in the print preview window.

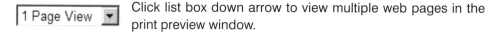 Click list box down arrow to view multiple web pages in the print preview window.

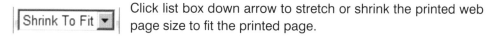 Click list box down arrow to stretch or shrink the printed web page size to fit the printed page.

Click this button to close the Print Preview window.

Print Preview – Navigation Page Bar

 Click this button to go to first page.

 Click this button to go to previous page.

 Click this button to go to next page.

 Click this button to go to last page.

Printing a Web Page

Print a web page which you have opened in your browser window as follows:

- Go to the File menu and select the 'Print' command. The Print dialogue box will now open.
- Click the 'General' tab and select the printer.

- Under the 'Page Range' section in the Print dialogue box:
  — click in the radio button to the left of 'All', if you wish to print all the pages
  — click the 'Selection' button if you wish to print an already selected selection of a web page
  — click the 'Current Page' button if you want to print the current page
  — click the 'Pages' button and enter page number or range of pages you want to print in the 'Page Range' box
  — use the down arrow to select number of copies
  — if you want to 'Print Frames' (frames are separate pages within the web page) select the Options tab and then click the appropriate radio button.

- If you want to print a picture from a web page, right click on the picture and then select the 'Print' command from the context-sensitive menu which will open. This command will open the Print dialogue box.

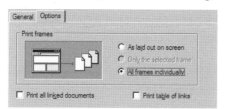

- Finally click 'Apply' and the 'Print' icon.

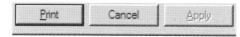

To save your web page to print at a later time:

- Click the check box next to 'Print to File'.

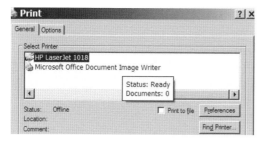

- The Print to File dialogue box will open.

- Select destination folder ('Save in:' list box).
- Enter file name.
- The default 'Save as type' will be shown as a printer file (*.prn).

- Click the 'Save' button.

Chat Rooms

A chat room (channel) is a virtual room on the Internet, where many people can chat, using text, to many other people simultaneously, usually on a specific topic or category, e.g. sport, business, science, art, law, etc. Some chat rooms allow you to upload images and music and use voice communication.

There are hundreds of chat rooms. Yahoo! and Google allow you the option of joining various chat rooms and they list the categories available.

A visitor to a chat room must first register and choose a password. When registering, a visitor will probably but not always choose an alias. Yahoo! encourages you to use their aliases feature, which will hide your e-mail address, protect your identity and prevent random contact with people you do not know or trust.

Once you have entered a chat room you can see a list of all the people who are available to talk to you. To talk to other visitors, just enter your text in the text box, and wait for a response. You can then have a 'conversation' or 'discussion'.

Tips for Safe Chatting

Don't chat about things that could enable a stranger to locate you. That includes your last name, the name of your school or workplace, the city you live in, and the places where you socialise. Be aware that not all chat rooms are monitored.

Protect your information. Don't put identifiable information, including photos, in your user profile. What's uploaded to the Internet can be downloaded and shared by everyone. Avoid posting photos that allow people to identify you. Yahoo! Chat is restricted to users who are 18 years of age or older (source: www.yahoo.ie).

Rules

- Chat rooms will usually list their rules.
- No spamming.
- Keep to the topic under discussion.

File Transfer Protocol

File transfer protocol (acronym FTP) is a set of rules that govern the transmission of files from one computer to another over the Internet.

Uploading web pages is discussed further in the Web Authoring section of this book.

- You *upload* files when you send or transfer files or folders held on your computer to a remote computer – an FTP server or site.

- You *download* files when you transfer files or folders held on a remote computer which acts as an FTP server to a folder on your computer. Your computer is known as the client computer.

An FTP site address (URL) can be entered in your browser's address bar: see the following example.

When downloading or uploading files using FTP, instead of using a browser that may have certain limitations, consider using a specialist FTP application, for example Classic FTP or Filezilla. Both of these programs are free and can be located and downloaded using a search engine.

When you log on to an FTP site, you may be required to log in with a user name and password. Anonymous FTP sites use the user name 'anonymous' and use your e-mail address as a password.

To open your FTP application, for example in Classic FTP:

- Click Start > Programs > Select your client FTP application.
- The main FTP window now opens. Click the 'Connect' button.

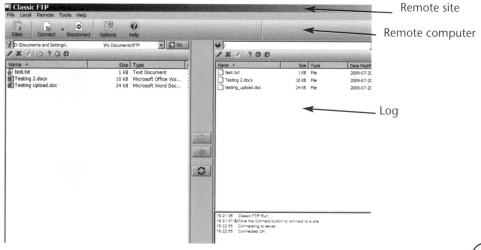

- A Login dialogue box will then open. Your host/server/site will have provided you with a user name and password: enter these in the Login dialogue box and then click OK.
- Click the down arrow to the right of the 'Connect' button to select the site you wish to connect to.
- If you have chosen to select the 'New Site' command, an 'Add New Site' dialogue box will open. Enter the specific details required in the appropriate 'FTP Site Properties' fields (if necessary access the Classic FTP 'Help' menu). Then click OK.
- To upload/transfer a file from a directory/folder on your computer to a remote computer, select the file or folder which will be displayed in the left-hand pane (local computer).
- Click on the 'Upload' button, the left to right green arrow.

- To download a file or folder from an FTP server or site on a remote computer to your computer, select the file, which will be displayed in the right-hand pane.
- Click on the 'Download' button, the right to left blue arrow.

- To end your FTP session, go to Menu > File > Disconnect Site.
- To close your FTP application, for example Classic FTP: go to Menu > File > Exit.

④ Security and Confidentiality

Introduction

Most people who access the Internet do so for legitimate purposes, for example transmitting data, e-mail, on-line banking, etc. but there are a tiny minority of people who for various reasons want to use it for nefarious purposes, ranging from the challenge of being able to beat the system without necessarily doing harm, to the other extreme where theft and the destruction of computer systems are the goal.

So when we access the Internet, visit websites, download files, etc. we have to be conscious of the threats involved and take the necessary precautions to protect ourselves. These threats can come from many sources, including:

- viruses/malware
- inappropriate content
- phishing
- spam
- cookies.

Viruses

'The Brain' was the name of the first virus ever created.[1] The date was 1986.

The term 'computer virus' was coined by Fred Cohen in 1983. His well-known informal definition is: 'A computer virus is a computer program that can infect other computer programs by modifying them in such a way as to include a [possibly evolved] copy of itself.'[2]

A virus can be described as a piece of code usually written to have a negative effect. It arrives uninvited and without your knowledge. It must piggyback itself on to something else, for example a piece of e-mail or another application. Viruses spread copies of themselves on a single computer.

Malware

'Malicious software (mal-ware) is a form of computer program designed with malicious intent.'[3]

Different Types of Malware

Worms

Worms are computer programs that replicate functional copies of themselves. Worms do not need to attach themselves to other files or programs. They can arrive via e-mail, and if they are opened they replicate themselves and then send themselves to everyone in your address book. Worms use network resources to spread from one system to another.

Trojan Horses

Trojan horses mask themselves as something desirable. They perform actions without the user's consent. They can change data, collect data and then send it to cyber criminals. They usually come in the form of an e-mail. They are launched when you open a program file or click on an action which will trigger the malware program. Trojans can arrive via Skype.[4] They do not replicate themselves but can take over your computer.

Keyloggers

Keyloggers record your keystrokes as you type them and are therefore particularly dangerous.

Spyware

This collects private information, without the knowledge or consent of the person whose information is being collected, and uses the victim's own Internet bandwidth to transmit the information.

Adware

Adware is similar to spyware but with one difference – the computer owner can inadvertently grant permission for its download by clicking OK to a licence agreement while downloading other software with which it has been bundled.

Protection Methods

Some ways of protecting your computer against an attempted virus or malware attack:

- Avoid opening e-mail attachments if you don't know who the sender is or if you are in any way unsure of the sender. Be wary of attachments with the extension .exe, .bat, .hlp, etc.
- Note that malware can travel on removable media, e.g. floppy disks, CDs, DVDs, flash drives, etc.
- Remember to log out of any site where you have entered personal information.
- Change your password often.
- Ensure you have an up-to-date anti-virus programme such as McAfee or Norton Internet Security installed on your computer. Perform regular scans and check that your anti-virus program is always on.

- Don't download files from a website unless you trust the owner of the site.
- If you think you may have contracted a virus and are running a virus protection program, for example Norton Internet Security, you can quickly run a scan by opening the Norton virus protection programme and then clicking on 'Run QuickScan'. Depending on the type and severity of the virus, you may be offered the choice to have the file quarantined, disinfected, removed or repaired.

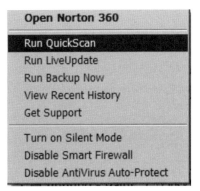

- Install a spyware program such as Skybot Search & Destroy.
- Backup your data. The best backup is a complete backup that can be restored to a new hard disk drive.[5] Your ISP may provide online backup service facilities.
- Be aware of the KRESV (Know, Received, Expect, Sense and Virus) test.[6]
- Use filtering software.

Filtering Software/Parental Control Software

Filtering software, or content-control software, is used to block access to websites which may be deemed inappropriate or objectionable. Some sites may contain images that are totally inappropriate for children, and as a result many people use content filtering software to block offensive websites. To protect children, do not allow them to access the Internet without an adult present as there is no totally effective censorship on the Internet itself.

Additionally, certain content on the Internet may be blocked by:

- internet service providers (ISPs), which can block URL websites
- governments
- schools or colleges
- parents
- employers.

Using Content Filtering Software

Content filtering programs are freely available. In Microsoft Internet Explorer you can create customised lists of acceptable or unacceptable websites by accessing its Content Advisor. The categories are indicated under the Ratings tab, for example, 'Content that creates fear or intimidation' or 'Depictions of alcohol and drug use'.

To switch on Content Advisor:

- Open Internet Explorer > Tools > Internet Options > Contents tab.
- Click on the 'Enable' button to enable Content Advisor. The Content Advisor window now opens.
- Click on the Ratings tab. Here you can set the ratings for different content types by using the slider.

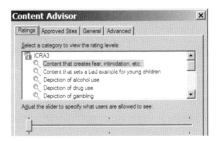

- Click the Approved Sites tab. To allow access to a specific website, enter the name of the website in the 'Allow this website' field, then press the 'Allow' button, then click OK.

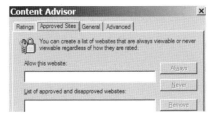

- To deny access to a particular website, enter the name of the website and then press the 'Never' button.
- Click on the General tab. If you wish to set user options:

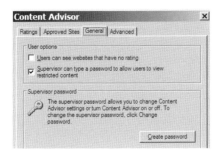

    — Leave the check box adjacent to 'Users can see websites that have no rating' deselected if you want to prevent users viewing sites that have not been rated.

    — Click the second option – 'Supervisor can set password to allow viewers to view restricted options' – if you wish to ensure that restricted sites cannot be viewed without entering a password.

    — Click on the Create Password tab to set a password. Click on the 'Apply' button, then click OK.

Pop-ups

Pop-ups are small windows that appear as separate windows when you view certain websites. They are used for advertisements and some are fine, but they can also be dangerous and when clicked can activate spyware.

You can add or remove pop-ups from specific websites as follows:

- Open Internet Explorer.
- Go to the Tools menu.
- Click on the 'Pop-up Blocker' command.
- Select 'Pop-up Settings'.
- 'Pop-up Blocker Settings' window will now open. Add or delete websites as appropriate.

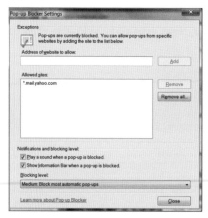

- Select pop-up 'Blocking Level' – high, medium or low.
- Click Close .

EXERCISE

- What is a virus?
- How are viruses activated?
- Name two different types of malware.
- How can you protect your computer from an attempted virus or malware attack transmitted over the Internet?
- If you think you have a virus, how would you treat it?
- When would you consider using filtering software/parental control software?

Firewalls

A firewall looks at the traffic coming into your computer or LAN from the Internet; it filters both incoming and outgoing traffic. The criteria used will depend on the type of firewall.

- It is a system designed to prevent unauthorised access to or from a network or from a personal computer.
- A firewall can protect private information held on your computer from an attack by an intruder.
- A firewall can be either software- or hardware-based.

Modern Routers

Modern routers often have a built-in NAT (Network Address Translation) firewall. These routers present your ISP's allocated IP address to the outside world while allocating an internal IP address to one or more computers in your home. The internal IP address is invisible to the outside world.

Microsoft Windows Firewall

There are commercially available Internet security suites, for example Norton Internet Security, which include virus protection, firewalls, etc. Windows XP Service Pack 2, Vista and Windows 7 have built-in firewalls.

- Check your firewall protection by clicking Start > Control Panel > Windows Firewall.
- Depending on the version of Windows you have and which view you are using in the Control Panel, for example Classic View (XP and Vista) or Category View [XP], etc., you can set your firewall security options by selecting either Windows Firewall or the Security Centre, or System and Security (Windows 7). To access the Control Panel

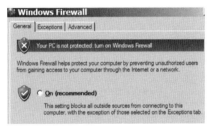

go to Start > Control Panel. The Control Panel window will then open. These options, among others, allow you to turn on or to turn off your firewall, or to 'set an exception to enable a particular program to send information back and forth through the Firewall' (source: www.microsoft.com).

Security – Personal Privacy and Identity Theft

It is essential that you protect your privacy when using the Internet. If you do not do so you may be vulnerable to phishing and spam.

Phishing

Phishing is a method of obtaining personal information, such as credit card and account details, by fraudulent means. This information could, among other things, be used to make purchases on your credit card without your knowledge. This is known as identify theft.

- Do not send personal information via e-mail unless it is encrypted.
- Remember: banks will not request personal information by e-mail.
- Monitor your accounts and erase all personal information from old computers before giving them away.

To check your phishing filter go to Menu > Tools > Phishing (Internet Explorer 7).

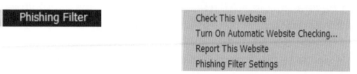

In Internet Explorer 8 the Pop-up Blocker is set through the Privacy tab: open Internet Explorer 8, then go to Menu > Tools > Internet Options > Privacy. Select 'Settings' and click OK.

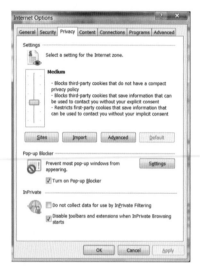

Spam

Spam is unsolicited e-mail that arrives in your e-mail inbox. Spammers may suggest, for example, that you have been specially chosen as the winner of an exciting exotic foreign holiday. Do not reply to spammers.

To avoid spam:

- Consider having a number of e-mail addresses, for example a public e-mail address for business use, a private e-mail address for personal use and a third for newsgroups.
- Check your junk e-mail settings. You can block or delete junk e-mail received from specific sites, and your e-mail client program will detect certain e-mail messages that it considers could be junk e-mail and send them to your 'Junk Mail' folder.
- Set up an e-mail address which contains both letters and numbers.
- Increase your e-mail security by reading your e-mail messages in plain text.

Reading Messages in Plain Text

To read messages in plain text in Microsoft Office Outlook 2003:

- Open Outlook 2003. Then go to Menu > Tools > Options. The Options dialogue box will open.
- Click the 'E-mail Options' button. The e-mail options dialogue box will open.
- Select the 'Read all standard mail in plain text' checkbox.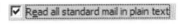
- Click OK to close the E-mail Options dialogue box. Click OK to close the Options dialogue box.

To read messages in plain text in Microsoft Office Outlook 2007:

- Go to the Tools menu and select the 'Trust Center' command.
- In the Trust Center dialogue box, select 'E-Mail Security'.
- Then click the check box adjacent to 'Read all standard mail in plain text'.
- Click OK.

Encryption

What is encryption ?

- Encryption is a means of scrambling information using a code that prevents it being understood by anyone who isn't authorised to view data.
- Files, e-mails and hard disks can be encrypted.
- Encryption is used in e-commerce and to secure wireless networks against unauthorised eavesdropping and spoofing.

Cryptography

- Public key cryptography was invented in 1976 by Whitfield Diffe and Martin Hellman.
- The keys are long numbers that act to scramble the data. Anyone with a copy of the key can read the data, but the message remains secret to those without a copy.

How to Use Encryption

- Both parties must know each other's public key.
- A public key is available to everyone and a private key is protected by and is only available to the owner of the key.
- When Peter wants to send a secure e-mail to Orla, he uses Orla's public key (which she will already have sent to him) to encrypt the message.
- Orla then uses her private key to decrypt it.

Secure Sites

Security Settings

You can alter your security settings in your browser as follows:

- Open Internet Explorer.
- Go to the Tools menu.
- Select the 'Internet Options' command.
- Click on the Security tab. Four zones are shown: select a zone to view or change security settings.
- Click on the slider to change the security level for the selected zone.
- Click on the Restricted Sites icon, and then click on the 'Sites' button.
- A Restricted Sites dialogue box now opens. To restrict a site, enter the URL for the restricted website in the 'Add this site to the zone' field box.
- Click Close to close the Restricted Sites dialogue box.
- Click OK to close the Internet Options dialogue box.

How can I Tell if a Web Page is Secure?

A secure website uses encryption and authentication standards to protect the confidentiality of Web transactions.[7]

To find out whether a website is secure, check the website's URL and look for the https protocol and for a closed lock icon.

Make sure that your Secure Sockets Layer (SSL) and Transport Laycr Security (TLS) settings in Microsoft Internet Explorer have been checked. To do this:

- Open Internet Explorer.
- Go to the Tools menu.
- Select the 'Internet Options' command.
- Click on the Advanced tab.
- Then scroll down to 'Security', look for the Web security protocols SSL and TLS and click on the check boxes next to 'Use SSL 3.0' and 'Use TLS 1.0'.
- Click Apply and then click OK.

Digital Signatures

You can add digital signatures to many of the Microsoft Office applications, for example Word, Excel, PowerPoint, Access and Outlook.

'Digital signatures are a way to verify that a file or an email message is really from the person from whom it supposedly originated and that it hasn't been changed.'[8]

In order to digitally sign a file or e-mail message, you first need a 'Digital ID', which is issued by Certifying Authorities (CAs), and then you must install it on your computer.

When applying for a Digital ID you will be asked to provide identification, for example a state-issued driving licence number or passport number.[9] When you have received your Digital ID you will then receive two keys, one entirely private and the other public. The technology used is known as public-key cryptography.

A public key is available to everyone and a private key is protected by and is only available to the owner of the key.

'. . . Typically, a digital signature (a digitally signed hash result of the message) is attached to its message and stored or transmitted with its message. However, it may also be sent or stored as a separate data element, so long as it maintains a reliable association with its message . . .'[10]

You can, if you choose, encrypt the contents of your e-mail messages. The cryptographic button for an unread encrypted e-mail message in Microsoft Outlook is shown as 🔒 .

Checking Digital Signatures (Microsoft Office Outlook)

Outlook attaches this icon to a valid digitally signed e-mail.

An invalid signature is shown as: [11]

Click on the icons to view detailed information.

A digital signature will help to give the following assurances:

- It provides signer and document authentication:
  — signer authentication is the ability to identify the person who digitally signed the document
  — document authentication ensures that the document or transaction cannot be altered as a result of the digital signature's invocation.
- A digital signature provides a means of electronically replacing a handwritten signature.
- Your digital signature has the same legal validity as a traditional (conventional) pen and paper signature.

Digital Certificates

A digital certificate is the digital identity of the certificate owner. [12] It is an electronic ID file that operates like a driver's licence or passport, an electronic version of an ID card or passport that is issued by a trusted, independent organisation (a Certificate Authority) such as Alpha Trust, VeriSign, etc. It is used to authenticate the validity of a website.

A digital certificate will include the following: a public key and the corresponding owner's name; the name of the Certifying Authority (CA); a serial number; the digital signature of the CA, the date of issue and the validity period, for example valid from 25/02/2010 to 26/02/2011.

To check a website's digital certificate:

- Go to the 'File' menu and choose 'Properties'.
- The Certificate dialogue box will now open.
- View details.
- Click OK.

Cookies

Cookies are small text files that are downloaded to your hard disk by many websites when you visit them. These cookies can come from the websites themselves or from the advertisements that appear within these sites. They can be used to keep track of your browsing activity. Some expire when you shut down your computer, and others remain on your hard disk drive until they expire or you delete them. Their expiration date will depend on how long the cookie has been programmed to remain on your computer.[13]

Some sites, for example My Yahoo!, use cookies to facilitate automatic registration logon and these cookies can be useful.

Other cookies may not be so desirable, especially those saved by banner ads, which might put your privacy at risk by tracking the sites you visit and then using this data for marketing purposes.

To view the details for the various privacy settings available for cookies, use the Help menu in Internet Explorer 7:

- Open your browser.
- Go to the Help menu.
- Select 'Contents and Index'.
- The Windows Internet Explorer window now opens.
- Click on the Search tab.
- Move to 'Type in keyword to find' and enter query in the query field.
- Click on the List Topics tab.
- Select 'Topic to Display'. Then click 'Display'.
- To close window, click on the X (Close) icon.

To view the details for the various privacy settings available for cookies in Internet Explorer 8, use the Help menu as follows:

- Open your browser.
- Go to the Help menu.
- Click on the 'Help' command.
- Then click on the 'Internet Explorer Help' command.
- The 'Windows Help and Support' window now opens.
- Enter query in search field.
- Click on the Search icon.
- Click on the appropriate option. A new window now opens (Vista and Windows 7).
- To close 'Help', click on the X (close) icon.

How to Manage your Cookies

Although some anti-virus programs include management options for cookies, you can protect your privacy and block undesirable cookies in Internet Explorer, as follows:

- Open your browser.
- Click on the Tools menu.
- Then click on the 'Internet Options' command. The 'Internet Options' window will now open.
- Click on the Privacy tab in the Internet Options dialogue box.

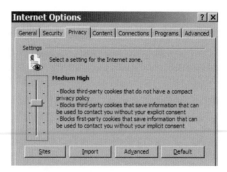

- Click on the 'Settings' slider to select your privacy setting. The default setting is 'medium'.
- Click Apply and then OK.
- Use the Sites button to specify sites you wish to 'Block' or to 'Accept'.
- Click the Sites button: a new dialogue box will open. Enter the Web address and select the option.
- Click OK.
- Should you wish to further refine your cookie settings, you can do so by clicking on the 'Advanced' button.
- The Advanced Privacy Settings dialogue box will open: select your options by clicking on the appropriate radio button in the Advanced Privacy Settings dialogue box.
- These options override automatic cookie handling.
- Click OK.

If you want to remove cookies:

- Open your browser, click on Tools > Menu > Internet Options > General tab. Select 'Delete Browsing History'.

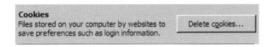

- The 'Delete Browsing' window now opens.
- Click the 'Delete Cookies' button.

- Click Close.

To view a list of cookies held on your computer, open Windows Explorer, then go to C:\Documents and Settings\User Name\Cookies.

EXERCISE

- Write a one-page note on the subject of cookies, explaining the necessity of managing them in the context of privacy.
- Useful source: http://www.w3.org/Security/Faq/wwwsf2.html#CLT-Q10

References and Resources

1   http://www.washingtonpost.com, 'A Short History of Computer Viruses and Attacks', compiled by Brian Krebs, 14 February 2003.
2   Ibid.
3   http://www.albany.edu/its/glossary.htm
4   http://www.cbc.ca/technology/story/2006/12/19/tech-skypetrojanvirus-061219.html
5   http://www.sei.cmu.edu/library/abstracts/news-at-sei/securitymatters3q03.cfm
6   Ibid.
7   http://kb.iu.edu/data/ahuq.html
8   http://www.us-cert.gov/cas/tips/ST04-018.html. Authors: Mindi McDowell, Allen Householder.
9   http://mcs.open.ac.uk/bp5/cert/

10   http://www.abanet.org/scitech/ec/isc/dsg-tutorial.html
11   http://mcs.open.ac.uk/bp5/cert/
12   http://www.arx.com/digital-certificate-faq.php
13   http://www.halifax.co.uk/securityandprivacy/howweremberyourusername.asp

(5) Electronic Mail

Introduction

What is E-mail?

E-mail is short for electronic mail. E-mail is sent over the Internet and is one of the most important uses of the Internet.

Different Types of E-mail

POP3 Client (Post Office Protocol)

A POP3 client (server) downloads all mail to the client computer, i.e. your computer, and removes it from the server. Most ISPs offer this service. Your incoming mail is held on the server's computer and when you check your mail, the mail is then transferred to your computer.

IMAP4 (Internet Message Access Protocol)

IMAP4 is very similar to a POP3 server, but this protocol allows you to view your e-mail without downloading it to your computer. You must delete your e-mails from the server. IMAP can be accessed from any computer, anywhere that has access to the Internet. You do need to check with your ISP to ensure they accept this protocol.

The protocol used to send an e-mail over the Internet is SMTP (Simple Mail Transfer Protocol). The protocol for mail received from your incoming mail server is POP3.

Web Mail

Web mail is accessed through your browser. The advantage of this option is that your e-mails are stored on your Web browser's server and can be read from any computer with Internet access.

Structure of an E-mail Address

An e-mail address, e.g. myname@yahoo.ie, has:

- a username (myname) – the local part of an e-mail address, or mailbox
- an @ symbol – which we can think of as a link between the user's computer and the host or server provider's computer
- the domain name – the name of the host or service provider's computer (yahoo), which is followed by a dot (.)
- the top-level domain (TLD), which comes after the dot. For example, ie is the country suffix for Ireland; com denotes a commercial organisation; gov is used for a government site.

EXERCISE

- Explain how e-mail and Web-based e-mail differ.

Setting up a Web-Based E-mail Account

Free Web-based e-mail services are available from:

- Google (Gmail)
- Mozilla Firefox (Thunderbird)
- Yahoo! (Yahoo! Mail)
- Windows (Windows Live Hotmail).

EXERCISE

- Compare the Windows Live Hotmail Web-based e-mail specification with that of Yahoo! Mail.
- Resource material: http://www.consumersearch.com

Setting up a Web-Based E-mail Account with Yahoo! Mail

We shall now set up a Web-based e-mail account with Yahoo! as our Web-based e-mail server or provider. Yahoo!'s Web-based e-mail service is called Yahoo! Mail.

Some elements of Yahoo! Mail's interface are similar to other e-mail applications. The account which we will set up is the basic version, which is free.

Yahoo! offers unlimited storage and integration with instant messaging (IM) services, for example Yahoo! Messenger and Windows Live Messenger. E mail attachments are limited to 25MB and accounts are de-activated if you haven't logged in for four months.

We shall be using Windows Internet Explorer as our browser.

First we must register with Yahoo! as follows:

- Open your browser window.
- Click the Start menu, and then click on the Windows Internet Explorer icon.
- Click into the address field in Windows Internet Explorer window, enter the Web address (URL – Universal Resource Locator) www.yahoo.ie in the address bar and then press the Enter key. The Yahoo! Ireland window will now open.
- Move to the right-hand side of the window and then click on the 'Sign Up' link.

- The Registration window will now open.
- Click into each field and enter appropriate data in the field boxes.
- Ireland may already be entered as the default country in the 'Country' field, but do check.

> Be aware that Web-based e-mail accounts will translate a fada in the surname field into coding, e.g. &#39

- Use lower-case letters when entering your Yahoo! ID, i.e. myname@yahoo.ie.
- Your Yahoo! e-mail address can contain numbers, but no spaces are allowed.
- You may not use punctuation except for periods/full stops – but you cannot use these at the beginning or the end of your username (myname).

- Passwords must contain at least six characters – these can be alphabetical or numerical.
- Type the code as shown in the text code field. This is a CAPTCHA entry code consisting of numbers and letters which can only be read by humans and not by machines. It is a measure used to prevent spamming.
- Click the check box if you wish to receive information on special offers.
- If you agree with Yahoo!'s terms of service, click the check box.
- Finally, click the 'Create My Account' button.
- Yahoo! will now confirm your account.
- Print the confirmation page and keep this document in a secure location.

EXERCISE

Register with Yahoo! Mail.

Using Web-Based E-mail

Our Web-based e-mail provider is Yahoo! Mail.

- Log on to http://www.yahoo.ie and click Sign In. The 'Yahoo! Sign In' window will open. Enter your user name and password and then click Sign In. The Yahoo! UK & Ireland page will now open.
- Select the Yahoo! Mail icon and then navigate to the 'Inbox' folder.

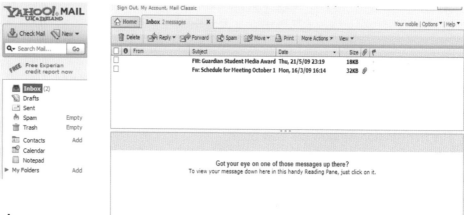

Inbox

- To check your inbox, click on the Inbox folder. Note that the unread messages are emboldened.
- To open a message, click anywhere on the message line. The message will now open in the 'reading pane'.
- Any attachments received with an e-mail can be opened by clicking on the file name. See example below.

📎 Schedule for Meeting - attachment.doc (21KB)

Important!

Do not open attachments received from senders you do not know or do not trust. This is a primary rule to help prevent your computer being infected by malware.

Opening Attachments

- Open e-mail.
- Click on the attachment file name, which is shown below the subject field, adjacent to the paper clip. The 'Download Attachment' window will now open.

- Click on the 'Download Attachment' button.
- The 'File Download' window will then open. If no virus is detected, click 'Download Attachment'.
- A new window now opens: 'File Download'.
- Click Save or Open; let's click Save.
- The Save As dialogue box now opens.

- Select the file location and enter the file name. Click Save.
- The 'Download Complete' dialogue box is then activated. Click Close or Open.

Replying to and Forwarding Messages

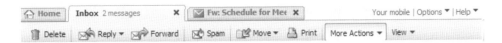

- Open the message and then click on the 'Reply' button. Click the down arrow and select 'Reply to Sender' or 'Reply to All'. A new 'Reply' window will now open.
- Click into the text pane to add your own message or comment. The recipient's address will already be entered in the address field in the 'Reply' window.

- To forward an e-mail, click the 'Forward' button. You must enter the recipient's address in the address field in the 'Forward' window.

Composing and Sending an E-mail

- Click the 'New' button.
- Enter the e-mail address of the recipient by typing the e-mail address directly into the 'To' field. Additional names should be separated by commas, for example, Jane Brown, Colm Brown.
- Add names to the 'Cc' field or the 'Bcc' fields as required. ('Cc' for carbon copy; 'Bcc' for blind carbon copy – the recipient can't see that you have copied the e-mail to a third party.)
- Enter the subject in the 'Subject' field.
- Click into the text pane and then write your text.
- Click the 'Send' button to send the message.

EXERCISE

Compose the e-mail message shown below and send it to your tutor. Send copies using the Cc and Bcc fields to your class colleagues.

> To all members:
> Please note our October meeting has been scheduled for 14 October 2011.
> Please let the secretary know if you are unable to attend.
> Thank you.
>
> Anna Moore
> Secretary

Compose and Save a Message as a Draft

- Compose a new message. Click on the Save Draft tab.
- To open a draft of the e-mail, click on the 'Drafts' folder.

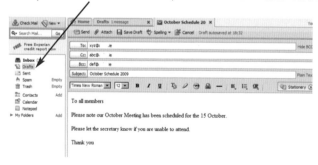

- Click on the draft you want to open. Click on the Edit Draft tab.
- Select the appropriate action, i.e. 'Send' or 'Attach'.

Attach a File

To attach a file (e.g. a Word document, a photograph or a spreadsheet) to an e-mail:

- Click on the 'Attach' button. The Choose File to Upload dialogue box now opens. Browse to the file you wish to attach and click Open.
- The file now appears in your 'Compose' window.
- To delete an attachment, click the 'Remove' button.

EXERCISE

- Create the following **Word** document.
    The schedule for our October meeting is as follows:
    Meeting is scheduled for 8:00 p.m.
    Date: 14 October 2011.
    Venue: Round Room, Chestnut House, St Stephen's Green, Dublin 2.
- Save the file to your external storage device as 'Schedule for Meeting.doc'.
- Compose and send the following e-mail message and include 'Schedule for Meeting.doc' as an attachment.
    Dear Philip
    I attach a proposed schedule for our October meeting. Do let me know if you wish to change the venue.
    Regards
    Anna Moore
    Honorary Secretary

Sending an E-mail

To send an e-mail, click the 'Send' button.

Printing an E-mail

Click on the File menu and select the 'Print' command. The Print dialogue box appears. Select the default printer and click 'Print'.

EXERCISE

- Print one of the e-mail messages in your inbox.

Address Book

The contacts list is an essential component of any e-mail system. The Yahoo! contacts list allows you to save comprehensive personal data for an individual. In addition to their e-mail address it also allows you to save other personal details: address, telephone numbers, etc.

To add a contact's e-mail address:

- Click on the 'Contacts' folder in the left-hand pane of the Yahoo! mail window. The 'Contacts' window now opens.
- Click the 'Add Contact' button. The 'Contacts Properties' window will now open.

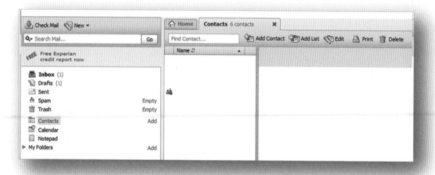

- Enter your contact's details and click Save.
- To close 'Contacts', click on the Close icon on the Contacts tab.

To edit a contact:

- Select 'Contacts', then select the contact's name.
- Click the Edit button, edit contact and then click Save.

To delete a contact:

- Select contact.
- Click the Delete button.
- Confirm deletion.
- Click OK.

EXERCISE

Add the following contacts to your address book:
- Alan Barber – alanbarber44@yahoo.ie
- Della Fitzgerald – dellafitzgerald79@yahoo.ie

Mailboxes and Folders

Mailboxes

A mailbox is where your mail is held on the server.

Folders

- There are five default folders – Inbox, Drafts, Sent, Spam and Trash.
- To these you can add additional folders. For example, you might choose to add a Personal Messages folder and a Business Messages folder.

To add a new folder:

- Click on 'Add', to the right of 'Folders' in the left-hand Folder pane of the Yahoo! Mail window. A new blank folder is now displayed in the folder list.
- Double click on the text 'untitled'.
- Enter the new folder's name, for example Personal Messages, in the 'Name' box.

EXERCISE

Create two new folders named 'Picnic' and 'Music'.

Moving an E-mail Message to a Folder

When you open a message there is an option to move it out of the Inbox and into a particular folder.

- Click on the down arrow next to the 'Move' button and then select the destination folder.
- You can rename or remove a folder by right clicking on the name of the folder.

EXERCISE

Move an e-mail message to the Music folder.

Help

To access the Yahoo! Help service, click on the Yahoo! Mail 'Help' button which is adjacent to the 'Options' button, in the right-hand corner of the Yahoo! Mail window, and enter your search criteria in the Yahoo! Mail search box.

EXERCISE

Using Yahoo! Help, find information on Folders.

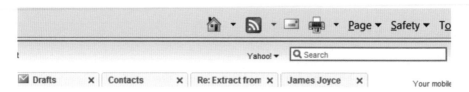

Search

The 'Search' field is positioned at the top of the Yahoo! Mail window, under the 'Check Mail' and 'New' buttons. This allows you to search all messages for a name or a word. For example, you might want to find all messages that have the word 'Christmas' in the subject line or all messages from 'Colm'.

EXERCISE

- Use the search facility in Yahoo! Mail to search your e-mail messages for the text 'Meeting'.
- Save this message to your external storage media as Meeting.doc

About Options

Yahoo! allows us to select our options/preferences for the way in which some of the features of the service work for us.

- Click on the 'Options' button and then click on 'More Options'. The 'General' window now opens.

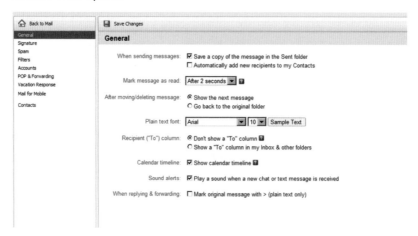

- Under 'General' options, we can save a copy of all out outgoing e-mail to the 'Sent' folder or we can request Yahoo! Mail to automatically add new recipients to our 'Contacts'.

To Exit a Yahoo! E-mail Session

- Close all open tabs.
- To sign out of the Yahoo! network, click Sign Out.
- This brings you back to the Yahoo! home page.
- Go to the File menu and select the 'Exit' command.

E-Mail Etiquette

E-mail etiquette – or netiquette as it is commonly known – is a matter of being considerate, aware and careful when communicating by e-mail.

The following are some factors worth considering when composing an e-mail.

- E-mails are not the same as a written letter; remember they can easily be forwarded to a third party.
- Always include the subject of the e-mail in the 'Subject' field. Some people just scroll through the subject line and then consider reading the e-mail at a later time.
- Keep e-mails short and precise. Most people don't want to read long e-mails.
- Keep lines to about 70 characters and keep sentences short.
- Do not write in capitals – in the electronic world this is considered the same as shouting.
- Although it is quite acceptable to use abbreviations, acronyms and emoticons in personal e-mails, try not to use them in a business e-mail: the recipient may not understand their meaning; and emoticons might confuse the recipient.
- Reply to e-mails as soon as possible.
- If you need to send a large attachment, first check with the recipient. Their application might not be able to handle large attachments.
- If you are replying to an e-mail, use the 'Reply' button. This will make it easier for the recipient, who can follow the thread of the earlier e-mail.
- Adding your name, position and organisation name to your e-mails will help the recipient to identify you.
- If you are representing an organisation, add disclaimers to your e-mails.
- Read your e-mail before pressing the 'Send' button: check content, spelling and grammar.

Discuss how you would improve the following business e-mail, with regard to its style, length and content. Consider:

- style – font and text
- length – e-mails should be short and precise
- content – relevance
- tone – friendly or formal.

> Subject: Meeting
>
> Dear Paddy
> I agree, we should meet at 4 to-morrow F2F.
> Could u let me know if this is possible? ☺
> BFN
> Charlie

Acronyms, Abbreviations and Emoticons

Acronyms

The Encarta Dictionary defines an acronym as 'a word formed from the initials or other parts of several words'. We are already familiar with acronyms, for example POP3, IMAP4, W3 (an acronym for the Word Wide Web), GUI (graphical user interface).

Abbreviations

The following is a list of abbreviations that you may occasionally come across in e-mails.

- BTW   – by the way
- EOT   – end of thread
- F2F   – face to face
- FAQ   – frequently asked question/s
- TTT   – thought that, too

Emoticons

Emoticons (a combination of the words 'emotion' and 'icon') are defined in the Encarta Dictionary as 'an arrangement of keyboard characters intended to convey an emotion, usually viewed sideways'. Emoticons are also known as 'smileys'. The following list shows the keyboard characters and their symbols.

- :-)   smile   ☺
- :-(sad   ☹
- :-| indifference   ☺

To find out more about emoticons, visit http://office.microsoft.com/en-us/help/insert-emoticons-HA001119608.aspx.

A list of acronyms and emoticons is available at: http://www.netresult.ws/cmoticons.htm.

EXERCISE

Complete the above list by adding another three acronyms and emoticons.

Using Windows Live Mail as an E-mail Client

Windows Live Mail is the current free e-mail client for Microsoft. It can be downloaded from: http://download.live.com.

To open Windows Live Mail:

- Open your Windows Live Mail application. The Windows Live ID window will open. Enter your user name and password, and then click the Sign In button.

Folder pane   Message information line

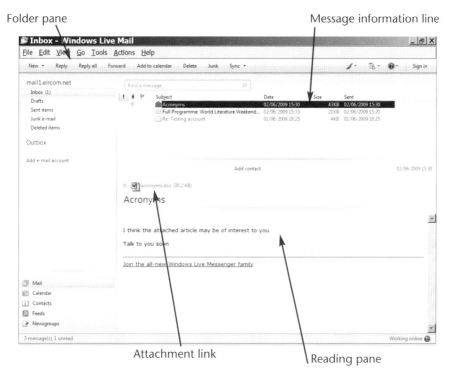

Attachment link   Reading pane

Checking E-mails

- To check your incoming e-mails, click on the 'Inbox' folder. Note that unread messages are emboldened.

- To open a message, double click on the message, and it will open in a new window.
- Any attachments received with an e-mail can be opened by double clicking on the attachment file link.
- Or right click on the attachment file link and select 'Open' from the drop-down menu.
- To save an e-mail, go to the File menu and then select the 'Save as' command. Save and then close the dialogue box which will have opened.

Replying

You can reply to the sender or forward a message to a third party as follows:

- Open the message and then click on the appropriate button. A new 'Forward' or 'Reply' window will now open.
- Click into the text pane to add your own message or comment. The recipient's address will already be entered in the address field in the 'Reply' window, but you must enter the recipient's address in the address field in the 'Forward' window.

Closing an E-mail

- Select the File menu and click the 'Close' command.
- To close Windows Live Mail client application, move to the Menu bar, select 'File', and then click on the 'Exit' command.

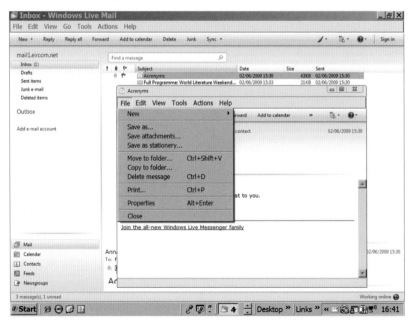

Composing and Sending an E-mail

- Click the 'New' button.
- Enter the e-mail address of the recipient by typing the e-mail address (e.g. def@yahoo.ie) into the 'To' box. Additional names should be separated by commas, for example, Jane Murphy, Colm Brown. Add names to the 'Cc' or 'Bcc' fields in the same way. ('Cc' means carbon copy; 'Bcc' means blind carbon copy – the recipient can't see that you have copied a third party.)
- Type the subject of the e-mail in the 'Subject' field .
- Click into the text pane and then enter your text.

To save the e-mail message as a draft:

- Select the 'Save' command (see below).
- Click OK.
- Close the new message window.

To open the drafts **folder:**

- Click on the 'Drafts' folder in the 'Inbox' window.
- Then click on the message. A new 'Drafts' window will open.

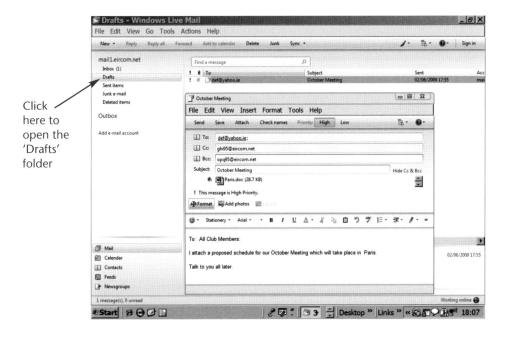

Click here to open the 'Drafts' folder

- To send the message, click on the 'Send' button.

To attach a file to an e-mail message:

- Open Windows Live Mail. Compose a new message, and then click the Attach button. See example shown below.
- The Open dialogue box will now open.
- Navigate to the file, then select the file and click on 'Open'. The file will now appear in the 'New Message' window under the 'Subject' line.

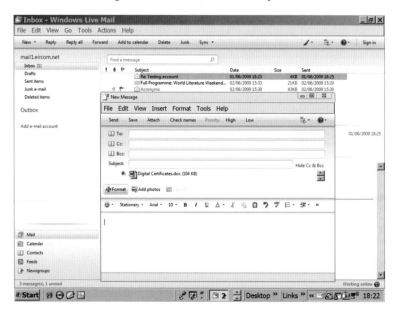

To remove an attachment:

- Right click on the attachment link, then select 'Remove'.

To send your e-mail: click the 'Send' button.

EXERCISES

1   Create the following Word document and save the file to your external storage device as 'Schedule for Meeting.doc'.

The schedule for our October Meeting is as follows:

Meeting is scheduled for 8:00 p.m.
Date: 14 October 2011
Venue: Round Room, Chestnut House, St Stephen's Green, Dublin 2

2 Compose the following e-mail message and add the 'Schedule for Meeting.doc' as an attachment. Send the e-mail to the e-mail address provided by your tutor.

Dear Philip
I attach a proposed schedule for our October Meeting. Do let me know if you wish to change the venue.
Anna Moore
Honorary Secretary

Address Book

The address book is an essential component of any e-mail system. The Windows Live Mail address book allows you to save comprehensive personal data for an individual. In addition to their e-mail address, it allows you to save other personal details, for example an address, telephone numbers, etc. In order to carry out the following procedures, you must have your Windows Live Mail application open.

To add a contact's e-mail address:

- Click on the 'Contacts' button in the lower left pane. The 'Windows Live Contacts' window opens.

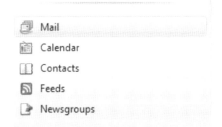

- Click the 'New' button on the toolbar.
- In the 'Add a Contact' window, select 'Contact'.
- Enter the contact's details.
- Finally, click the 'Add Contacts' button.

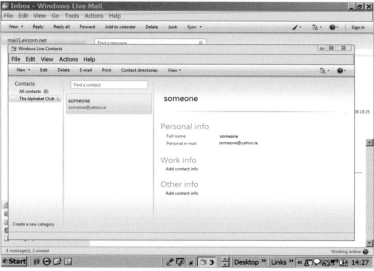

To edit a contact:

- Open the 'Contacts' folder.
- Then select the contact's name, e.g. someone@yahoo.ie.
- Click the 'Edit' button, click on 'Contact' in the 'Edit Contact' window and make your changes.
- Then click Save.

To delete a contact:

- Open the 'Contacts' folder and click on the contact's name.

- Click the 'Delete' button.
- Then click OK.

EXERCISE

Add the following contacts to your address book:
- Alan Barber – alanbarber49@yahoo.ie
- Della Fitzgerald – dellafitzgerald78@yahoo.ie

Mailboxes and Folders

Mailboxes

A mailbox is where your mail is held on the server.

Folders

- There are five default folders – Inbox, Drafts, Sent Items, Junk Mail and Deleted Items.
- You can add additional folders. For example, you might choose to add two folders: Picnic and Music.

To add a new folder:

- Go to the File menu, select the 'Folder' command, and then select 'New Folder' from the context-sensitive menu which will open.

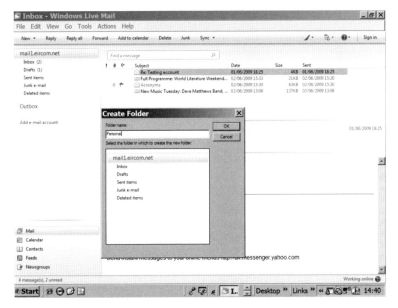

- A new window opens. Enter the folder name in the 'Create Folder' window.
- Click OK.

EXERCISE

Create two new folders named Picnic and Music.

Moving a Message to a Folder

When you open a message there is an option to move it out of the Inbox to a particular folder.

- Right click on the message, and choose 'Move to Folder'.
- The 'Move' windows now opens.
- Select new destination folder and click OK.

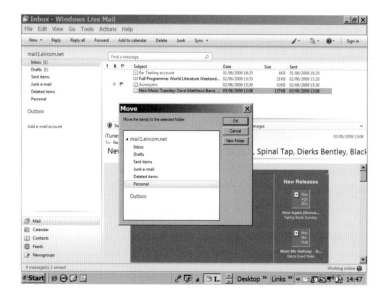

EXERCISE

Select an e-mail message and move it to the Music folder.

Help

To access the Windows Live Help service:

- Click on the 'Help' button, which is on the Menu bar. Click on 'Get help with Mail'. The Internet Explorer window now opens.
- Enter 'filter' as a search topic in the Search Box.

Search

To search for a message:

- Click on the 'Find' command in the Edit menu and select 'Message'.

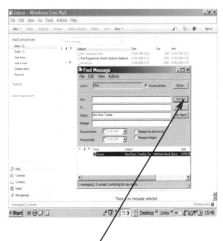

- The 'Find Message' window now opens.
- Enter the text in the appropriate field and click the 'Find Now' button. The results will be shown in the bottom pane of the 'Find Message' window.

About Options

To access Options:

- Click on tho 'Tools' button on the Windows Live Mail menu bar and choose 'Options'. The Options dialogue box now opens.
- Select the Send tab and click on the appropriate checkbox.
- Click Apply and OK.

Discussion Groups

Usenet Newsgroups

Usenet is one of the oldest communication systems available on the Internet. It was developed to allow people to discuss topics of interest through the medium of text messages or 'articles'. It can be accessed by anyone with a 'newsreader' or a browser.

The Usenet community is a distributed system and does not have any central organisation. If you want to access it though a newsreader your ISP has to host and share Usenet messages with other ISPs.

It is organised into a hierarchy of top-level groups, typically alt (alternative), comp (computer), misc, news, rec, sci, soc, talk. You can search through the list of groups hosted by your ISP. Eircom hosts nearly 30,000 newsgroups. To view a newsgroup using a newsreader (Windows Live Mail, for example) you have to join or, in the parlance, 'subscribe to' a particular group. For example, searching on 'dog' will return a list of all groups dedicated to our canine friends. Subscribe to that group and then you can view the threads for that particular group.

Once you have subscribed to a group, selecting that group in your newsreader will update the available articles, which are then available to read. To read an individual message or article, click on it and the message will be displayed in the reading pane (as with e-mail). To publish a post (reply) to the group, click on the 'Reply to Group' button, compose the message and then click Send/Post.

In recent years large Internet companies such as Google have hosted their own services. These allow access to the Usenet community and in addition Google allows us to form new groups outside the Usenet framework.

Electronic Mailing Lists

A mailing list is an e-mail-based notice distribution mechanism or a discussion group. Many of us will be familiar with the invitation to subscribe to a particular mailing list to be kept informed of new releases of software, etc. This type of mailing list doesn't allow reply or discussion.

Discussion-Based Mailing Lists

Discussion-based mailing lists have to be hosted by an 'owner', who maintains the list of e-mail addresses and allows 'posts' to the list to be forwarded to all names on the list. A subscription to a busy list can bring tens of messages per day into your Inbox. A typical topic for which there are numerous mailing lists is genealogy. For example, there are mailing lists for 'Moore' and for 'Dublin': you can post a question, e.g. 'Does anybody know of Anna Moore who lived in Ringsend circa 1900?', on both these boards, and wait for replies to the list.

Instant Messaging

Instant messaging, often shortened to 'IM' or 'IMing', is the exchange of text messages (chats) through a software application in real time. For IM to work, both users must be on line at the same time and the intended recipient must be willing to accept instant messages. You can then send instant messages back and forth instantaneously.

Voice over Internet Protocol (VoIP)

Voice over Internet Protocol is a technology that allows you to make computer-to-computer calls using a software program, e.g. Skype. VoIP has a number of advantages:

- the software is usually free
- there is normally no charge for computer-to-computer calls.

Short Message Service (SMS)

SMS is a mechanism used to deliver short messages over mobile networks. The message, which is text only, is sent from the sending mobile and is then stored in a central short message centre, which then forwards the message to the destination mobile. Each short message can be no longer than 160 characters (Latin alphabet), which can either be text or alphanumeric, e.g. 'See you tonight at 8:30 at our place.'

Blogs and Twitter

Blogs

A blog is a Web journal or a Web log. You can create your own blog, and listed overleaf are some sites where you can do so:

- www.blogspot.com
- www.wordpress.com
- www.livejournal.com.

Twitter

Twitter is a free service that lets you keep in touch with people through the exchange of brief messages, e.g. 'Meet you later'. See Chapter 1 for more details on Twitter.

(6) Web Authoring

Introduction

Before you can begin to make your own web pages, you need to understand how the Internet and the Web work. You should therefore carefully read Chapter 1 on the History and Structure of the Internet before starting this chapter.

What is the Internet?

When you connect your computer to the Internet it becomes part of a collection of millions of computers all round the world. These computers are all connected to each other and use the same set of rules to pass data between them. In the early days of the Internet, FTP (File Transfer Protocol) was the protocol used. However, this was found to be too slow for the Web and it could not cater for the latest features which Web designers wanted to include in their websites. A new set of rules called HyperText Transfer Protocol (HTTP) was agreed. This is the most common protocol in use.

There are two categories of computer:

- **servers** – the computers that store the data and transfer information that you request from the Internet via your computer
- **clients** – Individual computers, or end users, which request information from the network or upload data on to the network.

How Many Computers are Online?

The USA has the highest number of users per head of the population, followed by Oceania/Australia and Europe. However, Asia now has the fastest growing Internet population. The growth rate is slowing until broadband is further developed.

*Worldwide Internet Population**

2000	72 million
2004	934 million
2007	over 1 billion
2008	1.5 billion
2009	1.75 billion

*Statistics from the Internet Coaching Library

What are Websites Used For?

These are just some of the main uses of the Internet:

- **Communication** – the Web is a cheap method of communication. E-mail is replacing snail mail, and now you can send text messages to mobile phones over the Internet from your PC.
- **e-Commerce** – buying and selling on the Internet has become big business over the last few years. Anything from booking a flight, sending flowers, booking cleaning services, buying music and videos to ordering takeaway meals is available online, and numerous companies are involved in e-commerce.
- **e-Learning** – most colleges and universities have websites where you can find out about courses and apply online. Some colleges also facilitate online exams. Distance learning programmes, such as those run by the Open University, also use the Internet to communicate with their students. Teachers are able to upload student notes, assignments, etc. to school/college websites so that students can access them from any computer that is connected to the Internet. As well as providing greater accessibility, this facility will also hopefully reduce the amount of paper being used in education.

- **Information** – a huge amount of information is stored on the Web. You can research medical conditions or planning laws, find long-lost friends, etc. However, you should be aware that not all of this information is entirely accurate and you should be careful to visit several sites to check that the information tallies.
- **Social** – in the last few years there has been an explosion in the number of social networking sites on the Internet, for example chat rooms, message boards, blogs, YouTube, Facebook, Twitter, etc. This is probably the fastest-growing use of the Internet.
- **Downloading files** such as computer software and music files.

What do you Need to Access Pages on the Web?

- A PC with a modem and Web browser software (e.g. Internet Explorer, Mozilla Firefox).
- A telephone connection or broadband, or for a wireless connection, a PC with built-in wireless networking support or a wireless network adapter, a broadband Internet connection and a wireless router. The router converts the signals coming across your Internet connection into a wireless broadcast.
- An Internet Service Provider (ISP) – connects your computer to the Internet via the telephone system.

What is a URL?

A URL is a Uniform (or Universal) Resource Locator – an address on the Web. Each time you connect your computer to the Internet, a unique address is assigned to it. A URL must consist of at least two parts, but it can have many more. The first part of the address is called a protocol identifier: this specifies which protocol to use. The second part is called a resource name – it specifies the IP address or the domain name where the resource is located.

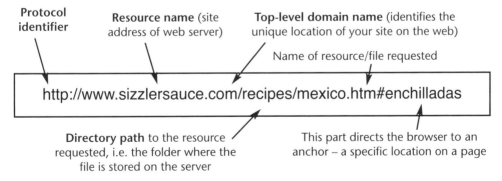

A domain name identifies the location of your website on the World Wide Web. The rental fee ranges from an annual fee of about €20 for a .ie domain name to €5 per year for a .org domain name. The domain name cannot be used by anyone else for the duration of the rental.

What is a Web Page?

A web page is a single document in a website on the Internet. A web page is not like a book with a fixed page size – there is no physical limit to its length. However, it is better not to put too much information on one web page, as users generally find scrolling tedious and lose interest in the content of the page.

What do you Need to Create Web Pages?

Hardware

- A PC with a connection to the Internet (either a modem with a telephone connection or broadband). If you work with lots of graphics you need a powerful computer with a fast processing speed.
- For multimedia web pages:
  — digital camera
  — scanner
  — microphone and speakers.

Software

- Text editor, e.g. Notepad.
- Web authoring software, e.g. Dreamweaver.
- Graphics program, such as Adobe Photoshop or Paint Shop Pro.
- Browser, such as Internet Explorer or Mozilla Firefox, which can be downloaded free from the Internet.

In order to upload your pages on to the Web you will need space on a Web server or host. Some Web hosts offer free space, but as nothing in life is really free, your pages will display a link to the Web host as well as advertisements which you might not wish to have associated with your site. Generally, the more you pay for your space, the more control you will have over the site. The Web host will provide your Web address and a password. Also, you may need file transfer software to transfer the files from your computer to the Web server.

What is the Function of a Browser?

This is the software (e.g. Internet Explorer, Mozilla Firefox, Google Chrome, Opera, etc.) that receives the data, interprets the HTML, and displays the results on the screen. You will also need to test your pages in the browser before you upload them. Different browsers have different settings, which can alter the way your pages are displayed. It is important, therefore, to have more than one browser installed on your computer so you can check that your pages will display correctly.

What is HTML?

HTML stands for HyperText Mark-up Language. It is a language developed to write web pages so that even if computers have different operating systems, they can still communicate with each other. This language (or code) formats the different parts of your document. The code is interpreted by the browser, which displays the results on the Web. This enables any computer connected to the Internet to view the formatted page, regardless of the operating system. HTML:

- is used to create web pages
- tells the browser how to display the web page
- is not a programming language
- is a formatting tool.

HyperText is text surrounded by code or tags which tells your browser how to display that text. An example of this code is:

```
<center><h2> <font color="#6A8455" face="verdana">
```

Eco Ireland

```
</font></h2></center>
```

This code (shown in purple above) will ensure that the words Eco Ireland are formatted as a heading in green, in Verdana font and centred.

Images and other objects such as videos cannot be pasted or inserted into a web page; rather the code creates a link to the location where the original image file is stored.

This code:

```
<img src="images/wicklow_mts_small.jpg"/>
```

tells the browser that the image of the Wicklow mountains is stored in the images folder.

HTML allows you to connect to places within a given document, to another page on the same website, or to a page located anywhere in the world on another website. It also allows you to navigate around a website in any order you wish, e.g. from page 1 to page 5, then to page 2, etc., rather than being forced to view pages in a particular order determined by the creator of the website.

Mark-up language is the code or tags – a system which identifies elements in a document, e.g. <p> for paragraph, <hr/> for horizontal rule, <div> for division, etc. These tags name the elements and have attributes, e.g. colour, size, face, width, height, etc. The attributes then have a value, e.g. 'green', '5', 'Verdana', '75%', '3'.

Shown below is an example of the code for the Eco Ireland index page.

```
index3.html - Notepad                                                    _|□|×|
File  Edit  Format  View  Help
<html>
<head>
<title>welcome to Eco Ireland's homepage
</title>
</head>

<body bgcolor="#E0EEE0">
<a name="top">

<table align="center" width="51%" bgcolor="#66CC66">
        <tr align="center">
                <td   "width-"17%"><b><font color="#FFFFFF" face="verdana"> <a
href="re_use.html">RE-USE </a></b></font></td>
                <td   "width-"17%"><b><font color="#FFFFFF" face="verdana"><a
href="recycle.html">RECYCLE</a></td>
                <td   "width-"17%"><b><font color="#FFFFFF" face="verdana"><a
href="index.html">HOME</a></td>
        </tr>
</table>
<hr color="#6A8455"/>
<marquee> <font size="3" face="comic sans ms" color="#6A8455">Everything you need to know
about the Irish environment</marquee></font>
<hr color="#6A8455"/>
<center><h2><font color="#6A8455" face="verdana">Eco Ireland </font></h2></center>
<hr color="#6A8455"/>

<p>
<center><a href="http://www.rhs.org.uk/advice/profiles0505/wildlifeponds.asp"><img
src="images/frog.jpg" width="400" height="303" border="0"alt="frog.jpg"></a></center>
</p>
<p>
<font size="3" face="comic sans ms" color="#6A8455"><center>our site is devoted to putting
Ireland at the forefront of the green revolution – our aim is to encourage everyone in
Ireland to minimise global warming and pollution. </center></font>
</p>
<p>
<div align="left"><font face="comic sans ms" size="3" color="#6A8455">These are just some
of the ways in which you can help</font></div>
</p>

<br/>
<br/>
<a href="mailto;eco_ireland@eircom.net">Email Us</a>

<center><a href="#top">Back to Top</a></center>
</body>
</html>
```

An example of how the browser would display the HTML code shown above is shown opposite.

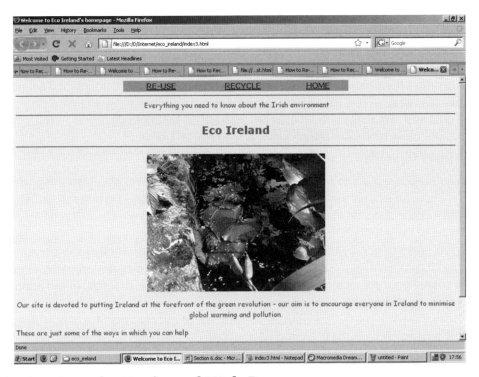

Evaluating the Design of Web Pages

When designing a web page or website there are some points you need to consider. It is a good idea to look at sites already on the Web and assess how successful they are. This will in turn help you to create better websites. Also, looking at existing pages and analysing them in a critical way, from both an aesthetic and a technical viewpoint, will help you avoid making classic Web design mistakes. Outlined below are a number of questions you need to ask yourself when analysing web pages.

Defining a Target Audience

Different topics will attract particular groups of people and a website must cater for their preferences, so you need to identify the target audience.

- Does the site assume that the user has a high or low level of Web experience?
- Does the site include multimedia files, such as audio and video files, which need particular versions of plug-ins for the user to hear or view them correctly?
- Is the site aimed at a particular age group, a particular nationality or ethnic group, or at people with a particular hobby or interest?

Suitability for the Audience

- Is the tone of the language used suitable for the target audience? For example, if the site is aimed at parents of young children the tone should be friendly and informal. If it is aimed at a profession such as medicine or law, the tone should be more formal and matter of fact.

- Colour schemes are very important and should be appropriate to the subject matter of the website, for example bright primary colours for a site selling children's toys, more restrained, subtle and complementary colours for a financial services site.
- Fonts and text styles should also be appropriate for the topic.

Purpose of a Site

- The purpose of a site affects its layout and structure. First establish the primary function, for example sharing information, social, education, commerce, etc. Does the website succeed in carrying out that function through the use of the navigation system, the information provided and other features such as interactive content?
- Web users generally take only a few seconds to decide whether the page they are viewing is of interest. Does the page attract your immediate attention?
- If so, did you look at the page long enough to take in the essential information or key sales message?
- Does the page make you want to see the rest of the site and, if so, did you take the time to click on the links and navigate around the site?

Technical Considerations

Layout

- Is the information well organised on the page, i.e. separated into sections with a navigation bar?
- Is the text readable against the background colour or image?
- Is the font size too small to read, with too much information crammed into a small space, or unnecessarily large and taking up too much room?
- Are there too many colours? Are they complementary or clashing? Are the colours very bright and glaring?
- Is the overall design pleasing to the eye and suitable for the target audience?

Graphics

- Are there too many flashing/animated images which distract the eye from the main message of the web page?
- Are the images of high quality, or are they pixelated? When an image has been enlarged and the resolution of the original is not adequate, you can clearly see the squares of colour – pixels – that make up the image.
- If the page takes a long time to download, this may be because the images have a large file size – you can check the file size by right clicking on the image and choosing 'Attributes' from the drop-down menu.

Ease of Navigation

- Are the links obvious? Most live text links on the Web are blue in colour and underlined, but some websites have dark or complex backgrounds and the link colour needs to be changed.
- Are the links laid out all together in their own section of the page?
- Can you navigate from the home page to all the other pages on the website with one click?

Linguistic Merits/Deficiencies

- Is the information given on the pages easy to understand? If the topic is a specialised or very technical one, is there a glossary of technical terms included?
- Is the language suitable for the target audience? For example, a site for tourist information should be simply and clearly written, and possibly available in several different languages.

There are many websites which can help you to evaluate the good and bad points of a web page by giving samples of both. Some of these are:

- http://designreviver.com/
- www.angelfire.com/super/badwebs/
- www.webpractices.com/

Designing a Web Page

Once you have completed your research, and decided on the topic, the next task is to gather information – text and images – that you wish to put into your web pages. If you decide to include text and/or images you have found on the Internet, or in a book, you must also include a reference or a link to the source of the text or image and you should contact that site to ask permission to use the material. Otherwise you are infringing copyright laws. If you are creating your own original photos or images, you should make sure to re-size and compress them to reduce download times. These topics are discussed in the Graphics Software section, page 158.

You can then begin to design the layout of each page. Consistency is very important in Web design, so you should choose a style for your site to suit the topic. The same style should be used for each page. The main tasks are:

Structure

- Create a file and folder system for the website, e.g. a main folder and, inside that, folders for image, audio and video files.
- How many pages will be in the site and how will they be linked together? Once you have decided this, you can draw an organisational chart to show the linking system. A simple example is shown overleaf.

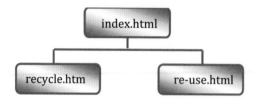

Layout

- How will the links be displayed? For example, they could go into a table, horizontally or vertically. When designing tables which will have images placed into them, you must be careful that the table cells are the correct size to accommodate the images. If you are re-sizing images, remember to do this in a graphics program before inserting them into the table.
- How will the information be arranged? You need to work out the numbers of rows and columns in tables, and how many tables you will need.
- If the other pages will be laid out in a different way from the index (home) page, this should be shown in a separate sketch.

A sample sketch might look like this:

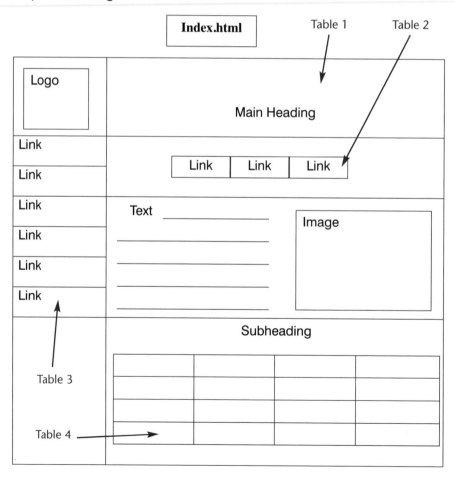

Choose a Colour Scheme

- Background colour for the page.
- Background colours for tables.
- Colours for text – headings, subheadings, body text, table text, etc.
- Colours for text or images to be used as links.

Create Style Sheets

Write down the specifications for each type of text you will be using – headings, subheadings, body text, table text, etc. These specifications should include the font face, size, colour and alignment.

Shown below is a sample set of style sheets.

Style Sheet for Index Page

Style Name	Face	Size	Alignment	Style	Colour
.mainheading	Verdana	h1	Centred	Bold	#CC0000
.secondheading	Verdana	h3	Centred	Bold	#660000
.tabletext	Verdana	12 points	Centred	Bold	#FFFFCC
.bodytext	Times New Roman	12 points	Left	None	#660000

Once these steps have been completed, the process of creating the website can begin.

Producing a Web Page

HTML

This section will cover the following topics:

- structure
- saving and naming a web page
- text formatting
- page layout
- inserting graphics
- links and anchors

- Web-safe colours and RGB colour system in hexadecimal
- lists
- tables and table planning
- comment tags
- special symbols and characters.

Web Assignment 1 – Ryan Family Website

Part 1: Make a Web Page

In this first assignment you will learn the basics of making a web page. The topics covered in this assignment will also be covered in greater detail in Web Assignment 2.

You will need to open three applications for this exercise:

- My Computer
- Notepad – Start > Programs > Accessories > Notepad
- your browser – Internet Explorer, Mozilla Firefox, etc.

Leave all three open, as you will need to switch from one to the other quite often.

Go to www.gillmacmillan.ie and search for *The Internet and Web Authoring*. On the *Internet and Web Authoring* page, click on the link in the right-hand column to access the support material. Copy the folder called **ryan** to your computer or memory key. This folder contains all the files you will need to create the Ryan family website.

First we are going to create the home page of the website.

Saving

Open the file called **index.txt**. Note that this is only a text file: we need to convert it to a web page. The easiest way is to re-save the page with a different file extension as follows.

Click on the File menu and choose Save As.

1	**Where?**	Make sure you are saving the page in the right location, so check that the **ryan** folder is displayed in the 'Save In' box
2	**What Name?**	Change the file name to **index.html**
3	**What File Type?**	Click the down arrow beside 'Save As Type' and choose 'All Files'

These are the **three important things** you need to remember when saving a Notepad file as a web page.

Structure

The HTML code of every web page has the same basic structure, as follows:

```
<html>
<head>
<title>
</title>
</head>
<body>
</body>
</html>
```

Note: for the purposes of this book, all html code is shown in Arial font and in purple to distinguish it from normal text.

Have a good look at this code and note that each tag, e.g. html, is surrounded by a left and right angle bracket, e.g. <html>.

Also note that each tag has an opening tag, e.g. <html>, and a closing tag, e.g. </html>, the difference being the forward slash in front of the closing tag name. There are a few exceptions to this rule, which we will look at later in this exercise.

Click into the top of the **index.html** Notepad file and type the head section of the code above the text that is already there, as follows:

```
<html>
<head>
<title>
</title>
</head>
```

Every web page has a title, which is displayed in the title bar when viewed in the browser.

- Insert this text in between the two title tags:
  Welcome to the Ryan Family Homepage
- None of this text will be displayed in the actual web page, however, so now we need to add the body opening and closing tags to the Notepad file:
- Type <body> underneath the closing head tag.
- And </body> at the bottom of the page.
- Finally type the closing </html> tag underneath the closing </body> tag.

Your **index.html** Notepad file should now look like this:

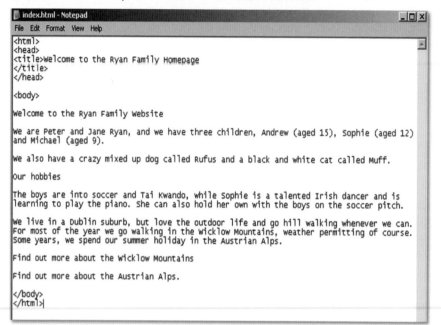

Check that your code is correct and save the page.
View the page in the browser:

- Click into **My Computer** and double click on **index.html**.
- The web page opens in your default browser (usually Internet Explorer).

Note that the title is displayed in the blue title bar at the top of the browser window and that the text is displayed in the web page without any formatting whatsoever.

The title is displayed in the Title Bar

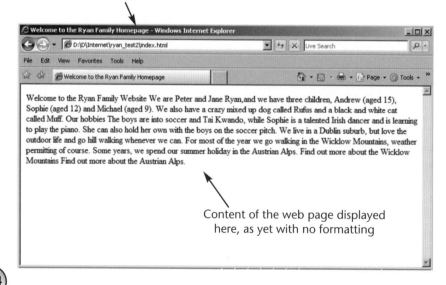

Content of the web page displayed here, as yet with no formatting

Part 2: Liven up Your Page with Colour

Now we will add some colour and format the text to make the page look more interesting.

> *Note:* don't forget to save the page. Click 'Refresh' in the browser whenever you make changes to the code to check that they are working.

- Open **index.html** with Notepad.
- In My Computer, right mouse click on index.html > Open With > Notepad.

Background Colour

To change the background colour, enter the following code in the opening `<body>` tag:

<p align="center"><code><body bgcolor="teal"></code></p>

You can replace "teal" with any of the Web-safe colours below:

Black	White	Blue	Teal	Olive	Green	Purple	Red
Gray	Silver	Navy	Acqua	Lime	Fuchsia	Maroon	Yellow

Save the page and refresh the page in the Browser. If you do not like the colour you have chosen, click back into the Notepad file, change the colour in the body tag, save and refresh as before.

Create a Heading

Next, format the main heading of the page by inserting opening and closing heading tags:

<p align="center"><code><h2>Welcome to the Ryan Family Website</h2></code></p>

Save and refresh as before to see the change.

Change the Colour of the Heading

Amend the code thus:

<p><code><h2><font color="white">Welcome to the Ryan Family Website</font></h2></code></p>

> *Note:* you only need to type *font* once in the opening tag. Also, the closing tag only needs the word *font,* you do not have to close the face or colour. Also note that the word 'color' is spelled the American way (without the 'u').

Change the Font Face of the Heading

Amend the code thus:

```
<h2><font color="white" face="verdana">Welcome to the Ryan Family
Website</font></h2>
```

Save and refresh as before to see the change in the web page.

Align the Heading

To align the heading to the centre, amend the code thus:

```
<h2><font color="white" face="verdana"><center>Welcome to the Ryan
Family Website</center></font></h2>
```

> *Note* the American spelling of the word *center.*
> Also note that when tags are 'nested', i.e. several tags are placed around one piece of text, they are closed in reverse order. In other words, *first opened, last closed.*

Create a Subheading

To make 'Our Hobbies' a subheading, amend the code thus:

```
<h4><font color="white" face="verdana">Our Hobbies</font></h4>
```

Insert Paragraphs

Create some white space by introducing paragraphs.

You can see that by using a heading tag, we have created some white space above and below the heading. The paragraph tag can be used to create two lines between sections of text, just as you would use the Enter key twice to create a new paragraph when typing in a word processing program, e.g.

```
<p>
```

We are Peter and Jane Ryan, and we have three children, Andrew (aged 15), Sophie (aged 12) and Michael (aged 9). We also have a crazy mixed up dog called Rufus and a black and white cat called Muff.

```
<p>
```

Insert opening and closing paragraphs where appropriate.

You can also use the <br/> tag to create one new line – this is the equivalent of pressing the Enter key once when entering text in a word processing program. This is a stand-alone tag, and therefore does not need a closing tag. However, to make it compliant with XHTML (see page 172) it must have a forward slash before the closing right angle bracket.

Insert a Horizontal Rule

Insert a horizontal rule underneath the main heading to divide up your page, using the code shown below:

<hr color="white" size="3"/>

Note that the <hr/> tag is a stand-alone tag, i.e. it does not require a closing tag. However, to make it compatible with XHTML, it must have a forward slash at the end and before the closing angle bracket.

Save the page again and check it in the browser. It should look something like this:

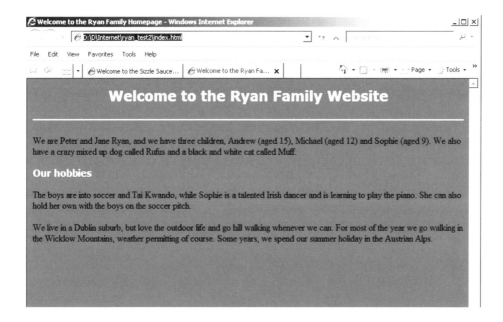

Part 3: Insert an Image and Make Links

Insert an Image

Inside the **ryan** website folder there is a folder called **images**, where the photo (**wicklow_mts_small.jpg**) we are going to use is stored. We must therefore include the name of this folder in the code to specify the correct path to the image.

The code shown below will insert the image **wicklow_mts_small.jpg** into the web page:

```
<img src="images/wicklow_mts_small.jpg"/>
```

The image tag is another stand-alone tag and does not need a closing tag, but remember to include a forward slash at the end of the tag and before the closing angled bracket.

Place the image tag in an appropriate position in the index.html page. To separate it from the text and create some space around it, use paragraph tags as follows:

```
<p>
<img src="images/wicklow_mts_small.jpg"/>
</p>
```

You can align the image by placing the *align* attribute inside the <p> tag, as follows:

```
<p align="center">
<img src="images/Wicklow_mts_small.jpg"/>
</p>
```

Make a Link

To make a link to another website (known as a remote link), the following code is placed *either* around text, e.g.:

```
<a href="http://www.visitwicklow.ie">Find out more about the Wicklow
Mountains</a>
```

(Use this code to make a text link to www.visitwicklow.ie)

or around an image tag, e.g.:

```
<a href="http://www.austria.info/au/nature-and-adventure-
austria/.html"><img src="images/austria_mts_small.jpg"/></a>
```

(Use this code to make the image austria_mts_small.jpg into a link to www.austria.info/au/nature-and-adventure-austria/.html)

Insert a Back to Top Link

This is known as an anchor link. It has two parts:

- First make the link at the bottom of the page. Enter the code shown below just above the *closing* </body> tag:

<a href="#top">Back to Top</a>

- Note the hash symbol in front of the word 'top'. This is very important – the link will not work without it.
- Now make the anchor for the link to jump to. Enter the code shown below just underneath the *opening* <body> tag:

<a name-"top">

- Save the page and check it in the browser. Note that the anchor at the top of the page is not visible. Also note that the words 'Back to Top' have become a link: when these words are clicked the page jumps back to the top. As our page is not very long, this may not be noticeable.

Part 4: Make Two More Pages and Link them Together

Make the Wicklow Page

- Open the Notepad file called **wicklow.txt**, which is stored in the **ryan** folder.
- Save the page as **wicklow.html**
- Copy the HTML code from the index page from the *opening* <html> tag to the *opening* <body> tag and paste it at the top of the Wicklow page.
- Inside the *title* tag, replace the word 'Home page' with 'Wicklow Page'.
- Type the closing </body> and </html> tags at the bottom of the page.
- Save the page again and open it in the browser by double clicking **wicklow.html** in My Computer to check that the page is correct.

Make a Link from the Wicklow Page to the Index Page

Click back into the **wickow.html** Notepad file and enter the following code just above the **closing** </body> tag:

<a href="index.html">Back to the Ryan Family Home page</a>

Save the page again and check it in the browser.

Make the Austria Page

Repeat the above process for the Austria page.

Tables

We want to make links from the Index page to the Wicklow and Austria pages and create a table to contain them.

Tables help lay out information in a grid formation on a web page. You can create a simple table with one row and two columns to contain the text links.

- Re-open the **index.html** Notepad file and enter the following text underneath the main heading:

```
<table align= "center" cellpadding= "3" cellspacing= "3">
    <tr>
            <td font face="verdana" size="4"> <a href=
    "wicklow.html"> Wicklow </a></font></td>
            <td font face="verdana" size="4"> <a href=
    "austria.html"> Austria </a></font></td>
    </tr>
</table>
```

The code for a table is `<table></table>`
The code for a table row is `<tr> </tr>`
The code for a column is `<td> </td>`

- Don't forget, you can format the text in the Wicklow and Austria pages with the same font face, colour and size as the index page, using the font tag.
- Save the page and check that the links work in the browser.

To make the pages consistent, you can now copy this code and paste it just below the main heading on the Wicklow page, but you will need to replace the link for Wicklow with the link for the home page.

Repeat for the Austria page.

You will now be able to navigate between all three pages without using the back button in your browser.

The finished Ryan Family index page should look something like the one shown opposite. The Wicklow and Austria pages should have a similar layout.

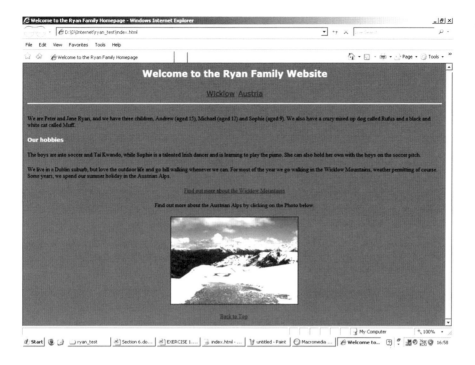

Web Assignment 2 – Eco Ireland

For this exercise you will need Notepad, Internet Explorer and My Computer. However, you do not need an Internet connection to view your pages in the browser.

Scenario

You have been asked by Eco Ireland to create a website for them. As discussed at the beginning of this chapter, you would normally spend some time planning the website in detail. However, the purpose of this exercise is to learn the basics of HTML, so you will be learning new skills as you build the site.

Before We Start

As with Web Assignment 1, go to www.gillmacmillan.ie, search for *The Internet and Web Authoring*, and copy the **eco_ireland** folder. Paste it into an appropriate location on your computer or memory key. The file/folder structure in the **eco_ireland** folder is very important to ensure that your links work and that the page uploads on to the Web correctly. Keep the My Computer window open – you will need it later.

Structure, Saving and Naming

Every web page must have the same structure, i.e. it must have Head and Body sections. The Head section contains the title of the web page, which appears on the title bar at the top of the window when viewed in the browser. The Body section is where everything you want to be displayed in the web page (text and images) must be placed.

Also note that all tags are surrounded by left and right angled brackets and nearly all have opening and closing tags.

- Click on Start > Programs > Accessories and choose Notepad. Type the following code exactly as it appears here:

```
<html>
<head>
<title>
</title>
</head>
<body>
</body>
</html>
```

- Save the page as **template.txt** in the **eco_ireland** folder. You now have a template, which will save re-typing this code when you want to make a new page. Each time you make a new page, open template.txt and then save it with a new name and with the .html extension.

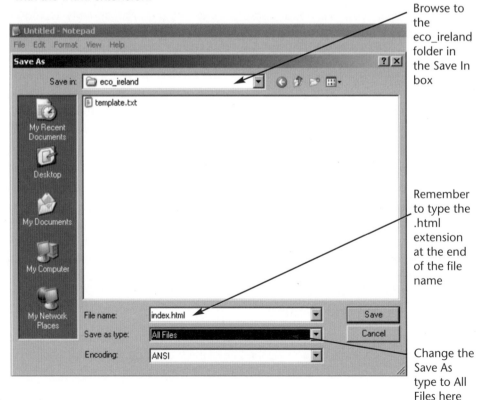

Browse to the eco_ireland folder in the Save In box

Remember to type the .html extension at the end of the file name

Change the Save As type to All Files here

- Now type *Welcome to Eco Ireland* between the opening and closing title tags in the head section.
- The top page of every website should be called index.html, so now save the file as index.html, click on the down arrow and choose 'All Files'. Make sure the **eco_ireland** folder is displayed in the Save In box, and click OK. This file is the home page of Eco Ireland.

Naming Rules

◆ No capital letters.
◆ No special characters – use only letters and numbers and the underscore or hyphen.
◆ No spaces.
◆ Keep web page names relevant and short.
◆ The index page (top or first page) of any website must be named **index.html**.

- Close the Notepad file.
- Maximise the My Computer window and double click on **index.html** in the **eco_ireland** folder. Internet Explorer opens and the web page is displayed. Notice that the web page is empty because we have not yet entered any text or images. However, the title is displayed on the blue title bar at the top of the browser window.
- In My Computer, open the file called **index_text** and copy the text. Close this file.
- Right click on index.html > Open With > Notepad.
- Click into the document and paste the text you have just copied into it between the opening and closing <body> tags.
- Save the page.
- Click back into Internet Explorer and refresh the page. The text will now appear in the web page.

Tip

◆ You can view the source of any web page by clicking on the View menu in Internet Explorer and choosing 'Source' (or right click on the page and choose 'Source'). The source code of the page is displayed in a Notepad file.

Formatting Text

Headings

- Heading sizes go from 1 (largest) to 6 (smallest)
- Code: <H1>Eco Ireland</H1>
- As well as making the text larger, this code makes the text bold and creates a space above and below it.

Font Size, Face and Colour

- Font sizes go from 1 (smallest) to 7 (largest).
- Font face – there are only a few fonts which are more or less Web safe, i.e. the majority of computers will have these fonts installed. They are Times New Roman, Arial, Courier New, Verdana and Georgia.
- Font colour – we will learn about the RGB hexadecimal colour system later, but for now we will use the standard 16 Web-safe colours that can be referred to in the code by name.

• Black	• White	• Blue	• Teal	• Olive	• Green	• Purple	• Red
• Gray	• Silver	• Navy	• Acqua	• Lime	• Fuchsia	• Maroon	• Yellow

An example of the code used to change the size, face and colour of text would be:

<font size="4" face="arial" color="purple">Welcome to Eco Ireland</font>

Note that you only need to type *font* once in the opening tag. Also, the closing tag only needs the word *font*: you do not have to close the size, face or colour. Also note that the word 'color' in the code is spelled the American way (without the 'u').

Font Style

Bold, underlined, italics:

- **Bold** – code: Eco Ireland
- <u>Underline</u> – code: <u>Eco Ireland</u>
- *Italics* – code: <i>Eco Ireland</i>

Now format the Eco Ireland index page text with font sizes, faces, and colours of your choice, and use bold, underline and italics wherever appropriate.

Page Layout

- *Break* – this tag creates one blank line (equivalent to pressing the Enter key once on the keyboard). It is a stand-alone tag, i.e. it does not need a closing tag. The forward slash after br is used to make the tag compliant with XHTML.

Code:

- *Paragraph* – this tag creates two blank lines (equivalent to pressing the Enter key twice on the keyboard).

Code: <p>Eco Ireland</p>

- *Horizontal rule* – this tag creates a horizontal line across the page, used to divide the page into sections. It is another stand-alone tag.

Code: <hr/>

- *Alignment* – left, centre and right. These tags can be used on their own, e.g.

<center>Eco Ireland</center>

or inside the <p> tag, e.g.

<p align="center"> Eco Ireland</p>

Note the American spelling of center.

- *Division* – indicates that enclosed content is a single block to be treated as one unit. This is essential for page layout. It is also useful for applying style sheet rules to a particular section of text. We will use it later for arranging a list and an image together.

Code: <div>. . .</div>

Now use these tags in the index page to make space between paragraphs, divide sections with the horizontal rule and align text.

Insert Scrolling Text

You can create scrolling text by inserting a marquee tag into the body section of a web page.

Insert this code underneath the links in the index page:

<marquee>Eco Ireland brings balance back into the Irish environment</marquee>

Save and preview in the browser – the text inside the tags will scroll across the screen in a continuous loop from right to left.

Graphics

Saving graphics to use in a web page:

- You cannot insert an image into a web page by copying and pasting directly from the Internet.
- You must right click on the image, choose 'Save Picture As', and save it into the **images** folder inside the folder where your Web page is stored.

The three image file types most widely supported for the Web are:

- **Jpeg** – used for photographic images. Can display up to 16.7 million colours.
- **Gif** – used for images that are not photos, such as cartoons. Supports animation and transparency. Can only display 256 colours.
- **Png** – an alternative to.jpg and .gif.

We will learn more about these file types later when re-sizing, compressing and manipulating graphics.

The code for inserting an image is:

<img src="images/filename.jpg">

Tip

- ◆ Note that the name of the folder where the image is stored has been inserted in the code in front of the image file name. This is because the folder is inside the main folder and the correct path to the image must be specified.

frog.jpg

- The *Alt attribute* should always be included when inserting a graphic. Alt stands for alternate (alternative) text; its function is to describe the picture in case the user cannot display pictures or for blind users who are using screen reader software. The code is:

<img src="images/frog.jpg" alt = "frog.jpg">

- You should *never* change the dimensions of an image with the height and width attributes, because the image will become distorted. However, you should check the dimensions of the image in your image editing program and then specify the actual size of the image in the code, so that it cannot be changed. The code is:

<img src="frog.jpg" alt = "frog.jpg" height= "421" width="600">

Hyperlinks

There are four ways of displaying a link on a web page:

- text (a word or phrase)
- a button (an image with text)
- an image
- a hotspot (also called an image map) where different areas on an image can be highlighted and these areas made into links.

You can join any of your web pages together with hyperlinks – these are called *local links*.

The tag used to create a link is known as an *anchor tag*.

An example of a *local link anchor tag* would be:

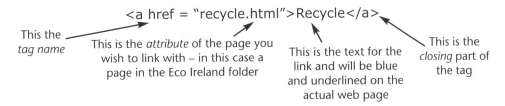

```
<a href = "recycle.html">Recycle</a>
```

This the *tag name*

This is the *attribute* of the page you wish to link with – in this case a page in the Eco Ireland folder

This is the text for the link and will be blue and underlined on the actual web page

This is the *closing* part of the tag

You can also link your page to other pages or sites on the Web – these are called *remote links*. An example of a *remote link anchor tag* would be:

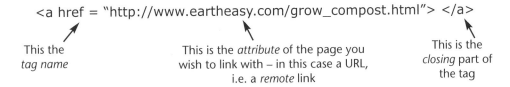

```
<a href = "http://www.eartheasy.com/grow_compost.html"> </a>
```

This the *tag name*

This is the *attribute* of the page you wish to link with – in this case a URL, i.e. a *remote* link

This is the *closing* part of the tag

Creating a Local Link to Another Page

First we must create more pages so that we can link them with the index page.

- Open the template Notepad file that you made earlier.
- Insert the text *How to Re-Use Old Stuff with Eco Ireland* between the opening and closing title tags in the head section of the page.
- Save it as **re_use.html**.
- Open the file named **re_use.txt**, select all the text, and copy it. Close **re_use.txt**.
- Click back into the **re_use.html** Notepad file and paste the text just below the opening body tag. Save the file and close it.
- Repeat this procedure to create the Recycle page using the filename re-use.htm.
- You should now have three web pages:
  — index.html
  — re_use.html
  — recycle.html

Create the links from the index page to the other two pages:

- Open **index.html** with Notepad and insert the following code just below the body tag at the beginning of the first line of the Eco Ireland index page:

<a href="recycle.html">RECYCLE</a>

- Save the page and preview it in Internet Explorer.
- The text <u>RECYCLE</u> will now be blue and underlined and, when hovered over, the cursor changes to a hand. This indicates that the text has now become a link. Click the link and the page **recycle.html** will be displayed in the browser.
- Return to the Index page Notepad file and insert the next link using the following code

<a href="re-use.html">RE-USE</a>

- Save the page and preview it in Internet Explorer.

Creating a Link to Another Website

- Type the following code just above the closing body tag:

<p><a href= "http://www.environ.ie/en/">Go to the Department of the Environment</a></p>

- Save the page and refresh it in the browser. *Department of the Environment* has now become a link: click it to go to the Department of the Environment website. Note that the full Web address, including the http://, must be included in the code.

Using a Picture as a Link

To create a picture link, place the two parts of the anchor tag around the tag used to embed the picture.

```
<p>Click on the image to go to the RHS website
<a href= "http://www.rhs.org.uk/advice/">
<img src= "images/frog.jpg" width= "400" height= "303" alt=
"frog.jpg"></a></p>
```

When you click on the picture of the frog in the wildlife pond, the RHS website advice page will open.

Tip

Make sure the picture you wish to use is in the same folder as the web page file and that you have used the correct spelling of the filename.

When a picture becomes a link, it is displayed on the web page with a blue border. Just as text links are underlined in blue, this is to let visitors to the site know that they are links. If you don't like the border that surrounds a picture link, you can instruct the browser not to display it. Add border="0" to the embedding tag, e.g.:

```
<img src="frog.jpg" border="0" >
```

The border will not show on the web page, but the pointer will still change to a hand when hovering over the picture to let visitors to the site know that it is a link.

Also note that img and src should not be separated. When you wish to add another attribute, type it after img src=". . ." and before the closing angled bracket.

The Named Anchor

A *named anchor* is used to create links that allow the user to jump directly into a specified section on a page, instead of having to scroll around to find what they are looking for. It is also known as a *bookmark*. A common example of this is a Back to Top link, which allows the user to jump from the bottom to the top of a page with one click. This is particularly useful if the page is more than one or two screens long.

• Insert the following code at the bottom of the Eco Ireland index page:

```
<a href="#top">Return to Top</a>
```

> ## Tip
>
> Note the placing of the hache key (#) in front of the anchor name – the link will not work without it. Also note that the anchor link and name are case sensitive and must be identical, otherwise the link will not work.

This code creates the link that, when clicked, will jump to the point on the page where you placed the named anchor.

- Insert the following code at the top of the Eco Ireland index page:

<a name="top">

- The anchor will not appear on the actual web page, but when the link is clicked the page will jump back up to the top.

Email Link

This creates a link to an email address and is usually placed on the contact page of a website, or on the index page.

Insert the following code in the index page in front of the words *Email Us*:

<a href="mailto:eco-ireland@eircom.net">

and place a closing </a> tag after *Email Us*.

Add More Graphics

In the re_use.html page:

- Insert the image called **veg_containers.jpg** and add the following text underneath the image:
- Plastic dustbins used to grow a mix of vegetables and flowers

In the re_cycle.html page:

- Insert the image called **recycle1.jpg** underneath the main heading.
- Insert the image called **recycle2.jpg** at the bottom of the page.
- Insert a Back to Top link underneath **recycle1.jpg**.
- Don't forget to include alt text in the code for the images.

Web-Safe Colours and the RGB Colour System

Hexadecimal Colours

Computing is based on binary code – a system which assigns either a 0 or a 1 to each piece of data or instruction, known as bits. Black was assigned to 0 and white assigned to 1. Originally, computers were designed to use a four-bit colour system, which limited the number of colours to 16. An eight-bit system was then created to allow the display of 256 colours.

Because these 256 colours could look very different on different platforms, e.g. Windows/Macintosh/Unix, an agreement was reached that 216 of these colours would be Web safe. (But you should be aware that even with developments in monitor technology and graphics cards, there will still be a difference with some of the colours on different screens, particularly with laptop monitors.)

To ensure consistency it was agreed that these colours would be specified using the RGB colour model: RGB stands for Red, Green and Blue.

Hex counts in sixteens, instead of tens, beginning with zero:

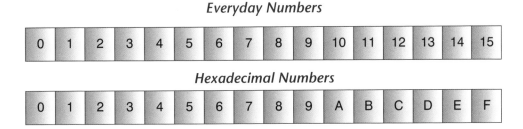

Everyday Numbers

Hexadecimal Numbers

Unlike paint, colours on a computer screen are made up of light, so when no colour at all is present, the colour will be black. Similarly, when the maximum amount of all three colours is present, the colour will be white. Some simple examples are shown in the table below:

Red		Green		Blue		Hexadecimal Number	Colour
0	0	0	0	0	0	#000000	Black
F	F	F	F	F	F	#FFFFFF	White
F	F	0	0	0	0	#FF0000	Red
0	0	F	F	0	0	#00FF00	Green
0	0	0	0	F	F	#0000FF	Blue
F	F	F	F	0	0	#FFFF00	Yellow
0	0	F	F	F	F	#00FFFF	Turquoise
F	F	0	0	F	F	#FF00FF	Pink

Experiment with the values of each colour to find a colour you like.

Background Colour

The code to create a background colour is entered inside the body tag, e.g.:

<body bgcolor="#808080">

This is the hex code for grey. Try experimenting with the Eco Ireland index page to find a background colour you like. Then adjust the text colour to make sure the text is visible against the background and that the combination is pleasing to the eye.

Lists

There are three types of list you can use on a web page: ordered lists, unordered lists and definition lists.

Ordered Lists – <ol></ol>

You should create an ordered list when the items in your list need to appear in a particular order, e.g. *Top of the Pops* top ten songs.
Each item in the list must have the <li> tag in front of it., e.g.:

```
<ol >
<li>Meat – will attract vermin</li>
<li>Cooked food – will attract vermin</li>
<li>Potato peelings – you'll have potato plants popping up wherever you spread your compost</li>
<li>Diseased plants/leaves</li>
<li>Woody material – unless it is shredded</li>
<li>Pernicious weeds, e.g. dandelion, creeping buttercup, dock, etc. </li>
<li>Weeds that have gone to seed – unless you can guarantee very high temperatures in your heap that will break down the seeds and prevent germination</li>
</ol>
```

Unordered (Bulleted) Lists – <ul>. . .</ul>

Use an unordered list for items of equal importance, such as items in a shopping list.
Each item in the list must have the <li> tag in front of it, e.g.:

```
<ul>
<li>walk or cycle to school or work</li>
<li>use public transport</li>
<li>if you have to drive a car, use an energy-efficient one</li>
<li>insulate your house</li>
```

```
<li>switch off electric appliances at source</li>
<li>use long-life light bulbs</li>
<li>use renewable clean fuels</li>
<li>buy local produce in season</li>
<li>buy loose/unpackaged produce</li>
<li>re-use glass jars, plastic containers, etc.</li>
<li>recycle only what you cannot re-use</li>
<li>compost kitchen and garden waste</li>
<li>create a wild area in a corner of your garden</li>
</ul>
```

Definition Lists – <dl> <dt> <dd> </dl>

Use a definition list for things like collections of words and their meanings, such as a glossary, e.g.:

```
<dl>
<dt>head</dt>
<dd>contains the page title, meta tags and CSS styles</dt>
<dt>body</dt>
<dd>contains text that appears on the web page when viewed in Internet Explorer</dt>
</dl>
```

- In the index page, format the list of 'ways you can help' as a bulleted list. In the recycle page, format the list of 'items not to compost' as an unordered (bulleted) list.
- Format the page with the same text and colours you used in the index page.

Tip

You can copy and paste the relevant codes from the index page.

- Insert the images **car_edited.jpg** and **cyclist.gif** above the list and align them to the right.
- In order for the text and the image to appear side by side we need to insert a <div> tag before the text, 'These are some of the ways in which you can help', as follows:

```
<div align= "left"><font color="#6A8455" face="comic sans ms"
size= "3">These are some of the ways in which you can help</font></div>
```

- Insert another <div> tag before the ordered list, as follows:

<font color="#6A8455" size=
"3">list</font>

(Obviously, if you have used a different font colour and size in your other pages you would need to change the code accordingly.)
- Repeat this process for the unordered list of 'items not to compost'.

Tables and Table Planning

Even though we have used the div tag to arrange the text and image on the page, the image does not appear exactly where we would like it to be. The next step, therefore, is to use tables to lay out our pages.

Tables are made up of rows and columns. A simple example is shown below.

Type	Item	Use
Plastic	Plastic dustbins	Growing vegetables such as tomatoes, beans, salad crops, etc.
	Yoghurt/margarine tubs	Sowing seeds and potting on young plants
	Transparent water bottles	Placing over tender plants in the spring to act as mini-greenhouses
Glass	Glass jars	Making jam, mincemeat; flower vases
Textiles	Old sheets, vests, etc.	Dusters, dishcloths
	Old clothes	Revamp by adding decorative ribbons, buttons, etc.

It is a good idea to draw the table on paper before entering the code – this can save a lot of time in the long run. You need to establish the number of rows and columns and where you need to merge cells.

Tables are set up using the <table> element with a closing tag </table>. Inside those two tags any number of table rows can be set up using the <tr>. . .</tr> tags. Inside these, the number of columns is defined by the number of data cells set up using the <td>. . .</td> tags.

In the re_use.html page, we will now create the table shown above.

- Open **re_use.htm** and type the following code between the two body tags:

```
<table border="1">
        <tr>
                <td>Type</td>
                <td>Item</td>
                <td>Use</td>
        </tr>
</table>
```

- Save the page and preview it in the browser. You now have a table with three columns, but only one row.
- You can now copy and paste the row (starting with the <tr> tag) six times to give you a table with three columns and seven rows.
- Change the text in each column to match the table above.
- Save and preview the page as before.

Merging Cells

To merge rows we use the rowspan attributes of the <td> element
To merge columns we use the colspan attributes of the <td> element.

- Insert the code:

```
rowspan="3"
```

  inside the <td> tag of the second row.
- Insert the code:

```
rowspan="2"
```

  inside the <td> tag of the sixth row.
- Save and refresh the page to view the effect this code has had on the table. The whole table looks a mess – this is because the first set of <td>. . .</td> tags in the third, fourth and seventh rows are now unnecessary and are creating extra columns. So remove these tags.
- Save and refresh the page once more. The table should now be correct.

Table Width

It is always better to specify the width of a table in percentages rather than pixels. This is because screen resolutions and sizes vary from monitor to monitor.

The width attribute is placed inside the <table> tag:

```
<table border="1" width="75%">
```

Cell Padding

This sets a space in pixels between the cell borders and the cell content. It is placed inside the <table> tag:

<table border= "1" width= "75%" cellpadding= "5">

Cell Spacing

This sets the spacing in pixels between the individual table cells. It is also placed inside the <table> tag:

<table border= "1" width= "75%" cellpadding= "5" cellspacing= "3">

Formatting Text in a Table

You can only format text in individual cells, so if you wish to change the text formatting in the whole table, you must place the font tag in each cell as follows:

- <td ><font color= "white" size= "4">Type</font></td>
- <td><font color= "white" size= "4">Item</font></td>
- <td><font color= "white" size= "4">Use</font></td></font>

Background Colour

Just as you can set the background colour of a table, by placing the code inside the tag you can set the background colour of:

- the whole table – <table bgcolor="black">
- a row – <tr bgcolor="black">
- a cell – <td bgcolor="black">

Return to the **re_use.html** page and create a table which will accommodate the two lists and the image. Give the table a background colour (different from the page background colour) and format the text accordingly.

Comment Tags

Comments are notes which you can place into the code of a web page to explain what your intention was when writing the code. If subsequent changes are needed, or if someone else takes over the maintenance of the website, comments help to clarify the original intention. Comments are also useful to mark unfinished sections.

Comments *only appear in the code* and *not* when viewing the page in the browser.

The comment tag is another stand-alone tag. An example of the code is:

```
<!- -this is the beginning of table 1. It has 3 columns and 7 rows-->
```

Add this comment above the table in the re_use .html page.

Special Symbols and Characters

There are hundreds of special characters, most of which are rarely used. Shown below are some of the most common ones:

Special Character	Code
Copyright symbol	&copy;
Euro	&euro;
Pound Sterling	&pound;
Ampersand	&amp;
At symbol (@)	&#64;
One space between two letters	

- Insert the copyright symbol at the bottom of the Eco Ireland index page, followed by your name and the date.
- Insert the space symbol ( ) between the hyperlinks at the top of the index page to separate them. Insert the pipe symbol (shift and the backslash key on your keyboard) between each pair of 's.

Web Authoring Software

HTML Editors

The main difference between an HTML editor such as Bluefish or HTML Kit (available as a free download from the Internet) and a WYSIWYG editor such as Dreamweaver is that with the HTML editor you are working with the code only and you therefore need a good knowledge of HTML. The editor writes the code for you, which prevents typing errors. Tags are inserted from a toolbar. However, in order to see how the page will display, you must open it from within the browser.

What You See is What You Get (WYSIWYG)

WYSIWYG software allows you to work in design view only, i.e. without showing any code, just as you would work with a desktop publishing program. You can also choose to work with a split screen with the code and design views visible at the same time.

FrontPage and FrontPage Express

These have now been replaced by Expression Web (May 2008, see below), but are still being used.

Advantages:

- The full version has some good features, e.g. a good Web graphics editor and FrontPage Explorer, which manages your site locally before updating it to the Web.
- It is easily available.

Disadvantages:

- It sometimes generates bloated code.
- It was not designed to handle pages generated by other Web authoring programs.

Microsoft Expression Web

- The major change is that most of the old FrontPage functions have been removed.
- Expression Web allows authoring of web pages integrating XML, CSS 2.1, ASP.NET 2.0, XHTML, XSLT. and JavaScript into sites.
- It provides accurate standards-compliant code, especially CSS rendering.
- Microsoft Expression Web provides the ability to install add-ons from third-party developers, extending the capabilities of Expression Web.

Dreamweaver

- Lets you place page content on different layers – like PhotoShop, this solves the problem of text alignment. Many people use it instead of tables, or with tables to allow exact placement of different sections on the page. However, layers can be unstable and do not always display correctly in different browsers.
- It has a range of independent floating panels, enabling you to organise your workspace efficiently.
- Dreamweaver is extremely successful because it supports every type of scripting and active content.
- In Dreamweaver CS4 there is now a Live View icon on the main toolbar which enables you to see a more realistic version than the normal preview of how the browser would actually render the page.
- The latest version of Dreamweaver enables you to use 'smart' PhotoShop images which automatically update whenever the original document is altered. This can be a great time saver.
- Dreamweaver's site management facility updates links on all the pages automatically whenever changes are made to one page. Again, a great time saver.

Introduction to Dreamweaver 8

This section is designed to give you a good basic knowledge of the Dreamweaver 8 program and to meet the requirements of the FETAC Level 5 Internet and Web Authoring modules. Should you wish to explore the full capabilities of the Dreamweaver 8 program, there are many resources, available both in bookshops and on the Internet, some of which are detailed in the References and Resources page at the end of this chapter.

The instructions given in this section refer to Dreamweaver 8. Only where there is a significant difference between Dreamweaver 8 and Dreamweaver CS4 are instructions given for both versions.

Getting Started

If a shortcut to Dreamweaver 8 is not displayed on your desktop, click on Start, Programs, Macromedia Dreamweaver, and Dreamweaver 8.

To open a new document, click on File, New and Basic Page in the Category section and HTML in the Basic Page section.

The Dreamweaver window:

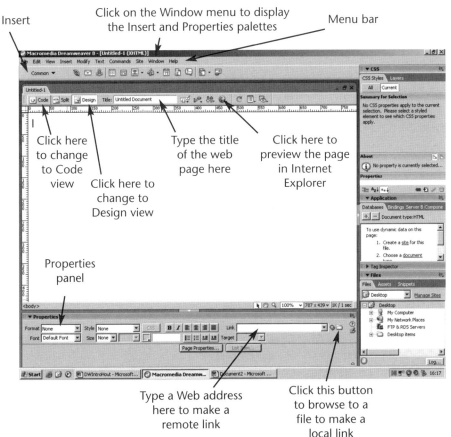

Insert

Click on the Window menu to display the Insert and Properties palettes

Menu bar

Click here to change to Code view

Click here to change to Design view

Type the title of the web page here

Click here to preview the page in Internet Explorer

Properties panel

Type a Web address here to make a remote link

Click this button to browse to a file to make a local link

If the Properties Inspector and the Toolbox are not displayed on the screen:

- click on the **Window** Menu
- click on **Object/Properties**.

The Attributes Inspector and the Toolbox are now displayed on the screen.

Note: The Attributes Inspector and the Toolbox are just two of the floating palettes which are available in Dreamweaver using the **Window** Menu.

Formatting text:

Use the formatting buttons in the Attributes Inspector to format the text, just as you would in Word.

Dreamweaver CS4

If a shortcut to Dreamweaver CS4 is not displayed on your desktop, click on Start, Programs and Adobe Dreamweaver CS4. To open a new document, click on the HTML tab under the Create New section.

HTML

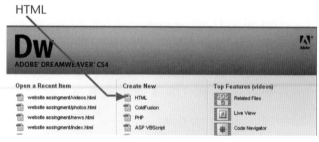

The Dreamweaver CS4 window:

Click on the Format menu to format text

Click on the Window menu to display the Properties panel

Insert panel

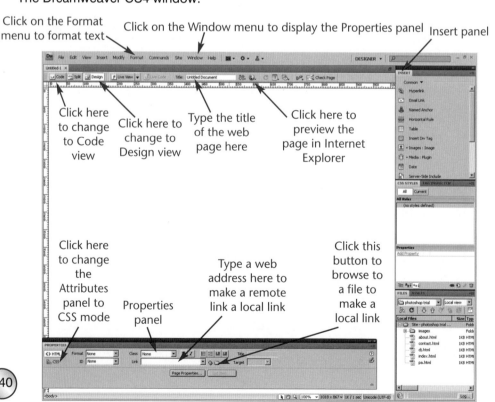

Click here to change to Code view

Click here to change to Design view

Type the title of the web page here

Click here to preview the page in Internet Explorer

Click here to change the Attributes panel to CSS mode

Properties panel

Type a web address here to make a remote link a local link

Click this button to browse to a file to make a local link

If the Insert/Properties panels are not displayed on the screen:

- Click on the Window menu.
- Click on Insert/Properties.
- The Insert/Properties panel is now displayed on the screen.

> *Note:* The Insert and Properties panels are just two of the floating panels which are available in Dreamweaver using the Window menu.

Formatting text:

Use the formatting buttons in the Properties panel to format the text, just as you would in a word processing program.

> Note that the Dreamweaver CS4 version formats text with CSS styles only. Instructions for creating CSS styles are given in the CSS Styles section below. These are the same for both versions.

Dreamweaver 8 Properties panel:

Dreamweaver CS4 Properties panel:

Changing the Background and Text and Links Colours

- Click on the Modify menu and choose Page Properties.
- Click on the down arrows beside Background, Text and Links. Select a colour, and click OK.

Creating Styles with CSS

Styles are used in web pages to keep the appearance of text consistent throughout. Using styles also keeps the code neat, as the code relating to particular types of text, such as body text, headings, subheadings, etc., is stored in the head section of the page. This avoids repetition in the code, thus saving time and effort. An example of this code is:

```
<style type= "text/css">
<!—
body {
        background-color: #FFFFCC;
}
.mainheading {
        color: #CC0000;
        font-family: Geneva, Arial, Helvetica, sans-serif;
}
```

Note: Dreamweaver displays the style sheet names in pink in the code.

Once this code is inserted into the head section, wherever you highlight a piece of text and select the style, in this case .mainheading, the style will be applied and will display thus:

Sizzler Sauce Company

The example above shows the code for one style only. However, many styles can be used in one web page. This is referred to as CSS, which stands for Cascading Style Sheets – the term *cascading* refers to the fact that many styles (known as style sheets, because they contain all the formatting for a particular style) can be stored in one web page. Web designers are now using CSS to control how a page is laid out and it is replacing tables as the preferred method of placing content on a web page.

- Click on the Text menu, then CSS Styles, and choose New Style. The New CSS Rule definition box appears. You can also access this dialogue box using the Styles Panel, which is displayed on the right-hand side of the screen.

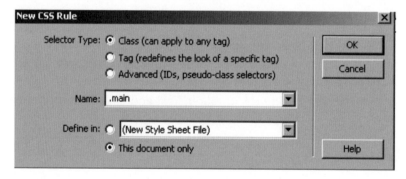

- Make sure that the Class option is selected and that the style is defined in This Document Only.
- Enter a name for the style in the Name box – the style name should *always* have a full stop in front of it and there should be no spaces and no capitals in the name.

- Click OK. The Style definition box appears:

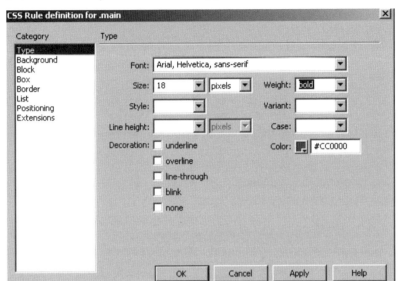

- Make sure that Type is selected in the Category list.
- Choose a font face from the drop-down menu in the Font box.
- Choose a font size, weight, colour, etc. and click OK.

To *apply* the style, highlight the text to which you wish to apply it, click on the Text menu and click on the style name in the drop-down list.

To Edit a Style

- Double click the style name in the CSS Styles panel. The Style definition box reappears; you can now edit the font size, weight, colour or face of that style.
    or:
- Click on the Edit Style icon at the bottom of the CSS Styles panel.

Saving

Before you can insert any objects or create links to other pages, you must save the page. The same rules apply when using Dreamweaver as when creating a web page in HTML – you must either save the image and the page in the same folder or specify the correct path. If you try to insert an image from another folder directly into the page, Dreamweaver will warn you that it may not display properly when viewed on the Web.

When creating a new page that may become part of a new website, it is a good idea to create a new folder for that page which also contains an images or resources folder. Then save or copy any images you might wish to use into that images or resources folder.

Making Links

Local Links

A local link is a link to a web page that is stored in the same folder as the current web page.

- Make sure the page has been saved.
- Select the text or picture that you wish to use as a link.
- Click on the down arrow in the Link box in the Properties panel.
- Browse to the folder where the web pages are stored.
- Select the web page file you wish to link with the current web page.
- Click OK.
- Preview in Internet Explorer.
- Click on the link to check that it works.
- Close Internet Explorer.

Remote Links

A remote link is a link to a page outside the folder in which the current web page is stored.

- Select the text or picture that you wish to use as a remote link.
- Click into the Link box in the Properties Panel.
- Type the full web address of the website you wish to use as a remote link, including the http://www at the beginning.
- Press Enter.
- Preview in Internet Explorer and click on the link to check that it works.

Creating a Link to a Specific Place in a Document

Named anchors let you set markers in a document and are often placed at a specific topic or at the top of a document. You can then create links to these named anchors, which quickly take your visitor to the specified position.

Creating a link to a named anchor is a two-step process:

1 First, create a *named anchor* – this is the location to which you wish the link to jump.
   - In Design view, place the cursor where you want the named anchor.
   - Click on the Insert menu, click on Invisible Tags and choose Named Anchor.
   - In the Insert Named Anchor box, type a name for the anchor.
   - If an anchor marker does not appear at the insertion point, choose View > Visual Aids > Invisible Elements.

2 Then create a link from another location on the page to the named anchor:
- Select the text or an image to create a link from.
- In the Link field of the Properties panel, type the hash key followed by the name of the anchor.

Tip

The link will not work without the hache (#) key. Anchor names are case-sensitive.

Inserting an Image

First you must make sure you have *saved the page*.

- Next, make sure the image is a suitable size and resolution – if you wish to re-size it, it is better to do this in PhotoShop before you insert it into the web page.
- Place the cursor where you wish the picture to be inserted.
- Click on the Insert Image icon in the Common Insert toolbar.

Dreamweaver CS4 Insert Panel

In CS4, the Insert panel appears on the right-hand side of the window, rather than at the top. However, the panel is basically the same as the Dreamweaver 8 Insert toolbar.

- The Select Image Source dialogue box appears.
- Browse to the file that contains the picture you wish to insert, using the down arrow in the Look In box.

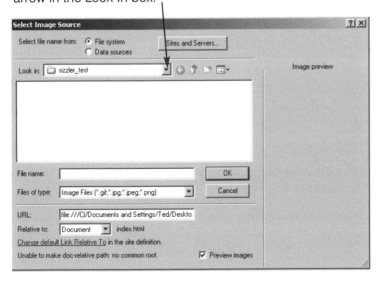

- Click on OK.
- The dialogue box shown below appears.
- Enter alternate text and click OK.

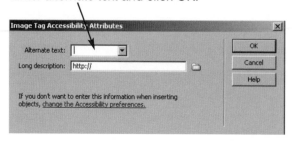

- The Properties panel now changes as shown below:

The width and height are displayed here

Click this button to browse to an image file and select it as the source

Click the down arrow to maximise or minimise the attributes

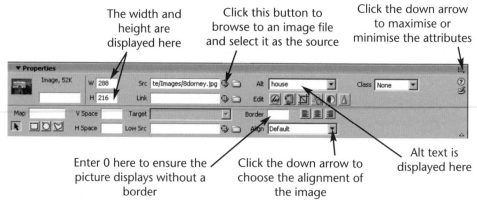

Enter 0 here to ensure the picture displays without a border

Click the down arrow to choose the alignment of the image

Alt text is displayed here

Note:
- Do *not* use the Text alignment buttons to align an image.
- Do *not* resize images in Dreamweaver, as they will become distorted. Resize in PhotoShop before inserting them into a web page.

Inserting a Horizontal Rule

- Click where you wish to insert the horizontal rule (a line across the page).
- Click on the Insert menu, HTML and choose Horizontal Rule. The Properties panel changes as shown below. You can change the width, the height and the alignment.

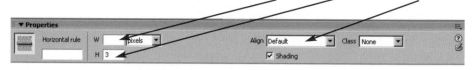

Note that there is no *height* attribute (to make the line thicker) for a horizontal rule in HTML; the code for this attribute is called *size*. If you switch to code view you can see that Dreamweaver has used the Size attribute.

Dreamweaver does not offer an option to change the colour. However, if you switch to code view you can enter the code yourself, e.g.:

<hr color="#FF0000"/>

The colour will not show in Dreamweaver, but will display when viewed in the browser.

Inserting a Table

- Click on the Table icon in the Common toolbar.

- The Table dialogue box opens.

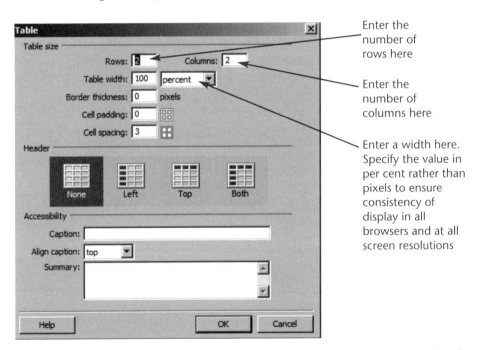

Enter the number of rows here

Enter the number of columns here

Enter a width here. Specify the value in per cent rather than pixels to ensure consistency of display in all browsers and at all screen resolutions

- Click OK when you are happy with the settings. The table is now inserted into the web page.

Selecting Cells

There are different ways of highlighting cells: click into the cell you wish to highlight and click on the td tag in the status bar; or click and drag. For the whole table, click on table, etc.

Editing Tables

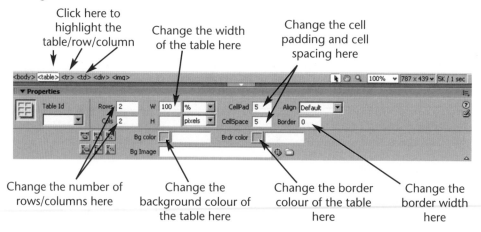

Click here to highlight the table/row/column

Change the width of the table here

Change the cell padding and cell spacing here

Change the number of rows/columns here

Change the background colour of the table here

Change the border colour of the table here

Change the border width here

- Changing the width and height – there are two ways to do this:
  — highlight the cells whose width/height you wish to change and enter the values in the width/height box; *or*
  — click the border of the cells and drag to the desired width/height.
- Merging and splitting cells – highlight the cells you wish to merge/split and click the merge cells/split cells icon in the Properties panel.
- Inserting columns/rows – highlight the column/row beside the one where you wish to insert a row/column. Click on the Modify menu, Table, and Insert Row/Column. Or click into the Rows/Cols box in the Properties panel and enter the number of rows/columns.
- Deleting rows/columns – highlight the rows/columns you want to delete and press the Delete key or click on the Modify menu, choose Table and Delete Row or Delete Column.
- Inserting images – click into the cell where you wish to insert the image. Then click on the Insert Image icon in the Insert toolbar and browse for the image in the normal way.
- Changing the background colour of a table/row/cell – highlight the table, click the down arrow in the bgcolor box in the Properties panel and select a colour.
- Changing the border colour of a table/row/cell – highlight the table, click the down arrow in the brdr color box and select a colour.

In **Dreamweaver CS4**, specifying the background colour/border colour of a table must be done with **CSS Styles** as follows:

- Create a style for the table/row/cell by clicking on the Format menu, CSS Styles, and choose New Style. Enter a name for the style, remembering to put a full stop at the beginning of the name.
- In the CSS Rule Definition box, click on the background tab in the left-hand panel.
- Choose a background colour.
- Click on the border tab in the left-hand panel and choose a border colour.
- Click OK.
- Apply the style to the table/row/cell by highlighting the table/row/cell and clicking on the down arrow in the Class box of the Properties panel.

Inserting a Comment

Remember, inserting comments is like making notes in the margin of a book. They are not meant to be part of the design or content of the web page: they are there as a reminder or an explanation of the design.

- Place the cursor where you wish the comment to be placed.
- Click on the Insert menu and choose Comment.
- Type the text you wish to enter in the comment, and click OK.
- Note that the comment does not appear in the page in Design view – switch to Code view to check your comment.

Meta Tags

Meta tags allow you to include special extra information about a web page that is normally invisible to visitors, but which can nevertheless be seen by browsers and search engines.

Search engines are specialised servers on the Web which catalogue and categorise web pages to produce a searchable database of Web content. Pages can be submitted to a search engine for inclusion in its database. Search engines also trawl the Web, following hyperlinks and cataloguing what they find.

Meta information is contained in the <head> section of the web page.

The <meta> tag requires two attributes:

1 The <name> attribute is used to specify the name of a attribute of the web page, for example keywords. The two most important attributes are:

- keywords
- description.

2 The <content> attribute specifies the value of the <name> attribute, e.g.:

<meta name= "keywords" content= "recycle, reuse, environment, ecology, recycling, green, energy, ireland, eco"/>

Keywords

Keywords are the words that a search engine would use to index your page. Any number of keywords can be included, separated by commas.

A page about cooking with chillies might have keywords such as recipes, chillies, hot, spicy, Mexican, Mexico, Indian, India.

There is no limit to the number of keywords used, but make sure these keywords actually appear in your web page and also try to imagine what the user may be searching for. They are not as important nowadays, as in the past Web designers tended to abuse them by repeating keywords several times to gain higher ranking in the list of sites stored in a search engine.

Example:

<meta name= "keyword" content= "chilli, chillies, pepper, peppers, hot, spicy, recipes, mexico, india"/>

To insert a keywords meta tag in Dreamweaver:

- Click on the Insert menu, HTML, Head Tags and choose Keywords.

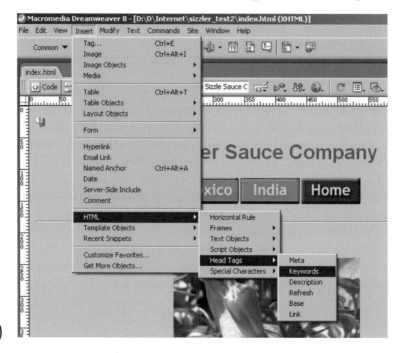

- Enter the keywords in the dialogue box as shown below:

- If you now check the code you will see the meta keywords have been entered just above the closing </head> tag.

The Meta Description Tag

The meta description tag is used to give a brief description of your site and what it does.

> ## Tips
>
> ◆ Keep your description short and relevant, but try to get across your unique selling point and make it interesting, so that the searcher will choose your site first, even if it is lower down the list of results.
> ◆ Make sure that at least some of the words in the description actually appear in the web page.

Example:

<meta name ="description" content ="Sizzler shows you easy ways to create hot and spicy recipes that will explode your taste buds "/>

Some search engines now ignore the description tag altogether and just display the first few words of your index page. You will need to register with a particular search engine before it will display your description in the search results.

To insert a meta description tag:

- Click on the Insert menu, HTML, Head and choose Description.
- Enter your description in the Description box and click OK.
- Check the code to see your description in the <head> section.

Imagemaps

An *imagemap* is used to create 'hotspots' in a graphic which are linked to different URLs. In HTML there are two kinds of imagemap:

1 **Server-side**. The actual link information is held on the remote server and this tends to lead to a slower response and download time
2 **Client-side**. All the relevant information is coded into the web page. This provides greater control over the appearance of the imagemap.

We will be using client-side imagemaps.

Once an image has been made into an imagemap, when you move your pointer across the graphic different URLs appear at the bottom of your screen. These are the URLs to which the hotspots are linked. When you click your mouse on the hotspot the browser goes to the new URL.

An imagemap is made up of a grid of points. The grid is made up of tighter or looser points, depending on the size and resolution of the image. It is therefore very difficult to pinpoint the co-ordinates of the area you wish to make into a hotspot, particularly if the shape is irregular – unless you are a mathematical genius! However, Dreamweaver comes to our rescue and makes image mapping easy. There are many other programs which can make imagemaps, some of which can be downloaded free from the Internet, including Easy HTML and MapEdit.

- Open a new Dreamweaver page.
- **Important** – save the page.
- Insert the image you wish to make into a map.
- Click on the image to select it.
- Dreamweaver will call the map 'map' unless you type another word into the map name box.
- Decide which area you wish to make into a hotspot.
- Click on one of the three selection tools at the bottom of the Properties panel, depending on the shape of the hotspot.

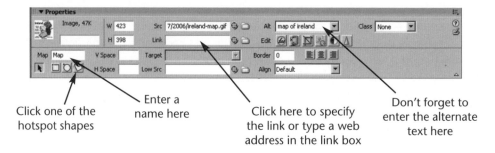

Click one of the hotspot shapes

Enter a name here

Click here to specify the link or type a web address in the link box

Don't forget to enter the alternate text here

- Click and drag on the image to select the hotspot.
- Click into the Link box in the Properties panel, and type the address/location of the page to which you wish to link the hotspot, or click the yellow browse button and navigate to the page.

- Make sure to enter appropriate alternate text in the Alt box.
- Make further selections if you wish and type each link into the Link box.
- Save the page again.
- Preview in Internet Explorer to check that the links work.

Define a Site with Dreamweaver

A feature of Dreamweaver is that it allows you to manage all the files associated with a website. Ideally a site should be defined at the start of the process of creating a website, but it can also be done afterwards.

- Create a folder for your site.
- Click on Site, New Site. The Site Definition box appears. Enter an appropriate name for the site. Click Next.
- Check that the button beside 'No, I do not want to use server technology' is ticked and click Next.
- Click on the yellow browse button and navigate to the folder you have created for your site. Click Next.
- If you have not yet set up your connection to a Web host, click the down arrow beside 'How do you connect to your remote server?' and choose None. You can set this up later. Click Next.
- Dreamweaver now gives you a summary of your site. If you are happy with the settings, click Done. The site is now created.
- Create the pages for your site, one of which must be named as index.html.
- Then create the links between the pages
- Set index.html as the Home Page: in the Files Panel, right click on the index page and select Set as Home page.

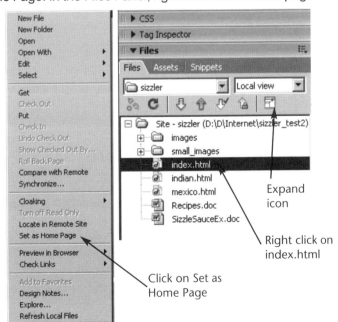

Expand icon

Right click on index.html

Click on Set as Home Page

The Expanded Files panel looks like this:

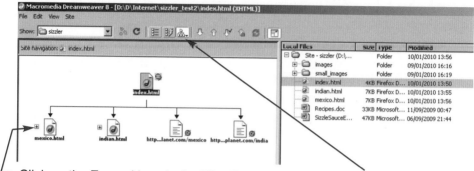

- Click on the Expand icon in the Files Panel, and click on the Map icon.
- Choose Map and Files to see the site map that Dreamweaver has created.
- The plus signs beside each page indicate a link – click on the plus symbol to show the linked pages.

Dreamweaver CS4:

Note that in Dreamweaver CS4, once you have specified the root folder and default images folder in the Site Definition box and clicked OK, the site is set up and the files are displayed in the Files panel.

Also, there is no option to set the home page – this is done automatically by the program. There is no site map displayed in the expanded Files panel.

Dreamweaver Exercise – Sizzler Sauce

Scenario

The **Sizzler Sauce Company** has asked you to make a website for them. They want the website to promote recipes using chillies. They have provided images and text. They need a home page and two other pages called:

- mexican.html
- indian.html

The Project

Using the Dreamweaver 8 program, create a website using colours you think will work well with the chilli idea.

As before, go to www.gillmacmillan.ie and search for *The Internet and Web Authoring*. Copy the **sizzler** folder from the disk on to your computer or memory key. Leave My Computer open, so that you can access the folder easily.

1 Create the Index Page

- Open a new html document, choose a background colour and a text colour, size and font face.
- Enter 'Welcome to Sizzler Sauce Home page' in the title box.
- Open the **index_text** Notepad file and copy it. Making sure you are in Design view, paste the text into the index page.
- Save the page as **index.html** into the **sizzler** folder.
- Create a CSS style called **.main** to format the heading 'Sizzler Sauce Company'. Create a second CSS style called **.subheading**. You will be applying this to subheadings in the other pages.
- Insert a horizontal rule just below the main heading.

2 Make a Second Page

You can make a second page by resaving the current one with a different name. That way you will not have to redo the background and text colours and the heading style.

- Resave the index page as **mexico.html**
- Change the title to Sizzler Sauce Mexican Recipes and save the page again.
- Delete all the text except the main heading.
- Copy the text from the **mexico** Notepad file and paste it below the horizontal rule into the Dreamweaver **mexico.html** page in Design view.
- Format the ingredients in the two recipes as bulleted (unordered) lists.

3 Make a Third Page

Make the **india** page in the same way, by re-saving the page with a different name using the filename **india.html** and changing the title as appropriate.

4 Links – Table

Make a table navigation menu for the links to the other pages:

- Return to the **index** page.
- Insert a table at the bottom of the page with one row and two columns and a width of 50%.
- Cut the text **Mexican** and paste it into the first column of the table.
- Cut the text **Indian** and paste it into the second column of the table.
- Insert another column into the table and type the text **Home** into it.
- Create a CSS style to specify font face, colour and size for the text in the table, which is going to be made into links. When choosing colours for the background of the table and the text, you must remember that links will be displayed in blue unless you change this in the Page Properties in the Modify menu.

5 Links – Imagemap

Use an imagemap to create a navigation bar for the links. Another way to create a navigation menu is to use a graphic which you can turn into an imagemap:

- Insert **navbar.jpg** at the bottom of the index page, and make sure it is highlighted.
- Click on the rectangular imagemap tool to create a hotspot around the word 'Mexico' and enter mexico.html in the link box.
- Repeat with the word 'India'.
- The Home button can be left as it is as you are already on the home page.
- Save the page and preview in the Browser.
- If you prefer the look of this navigation menu to the one you made in the table above, you can now delete the table.
- To make the pages consistent you should now insert the **navbar** image into the Mexico and India pages and create the relevant hotspots. You can then skip No. 6 Make Local Links and continue with No. 7.
- If you decide to keep the table, continue with No. 6.

6 Make Local Links

- Highlight the text in the first column of the table (Mexican) and create a link to the Mexican page. Do the same for the second column (Indian). Do not make Home into a link, as we are already on the home (index) page.
- Save the page, preview it in the browser and check that the links work.
- When all the links are working, copy the table and paste it into the other two pages. In the Mexico page, do not make Mexico into a link, but make Home into a link to the index page. Do the same for the India page.

7 Make Remote Links

- In the index page, highlight the text **BBC recipes** and make a link to the BBC website http://www.bbc.co.uk/food/recipes/
- Highlight the text **Good Chili Recipes** and make a link to the website http://www.goodchilirecipes.com
- Highlight the text **Email Us** and create an email link, using sizzler@eircom.net as the email address.
- Save the page, preview it in the browser and check that the links work.

8 Make an Anchor Link

- Type the text 'Back to Top' at the bottom of the page, highlight it, click into the link box in the Properties panel and type #top. *Note:* the hash key in front of the word 'top' is very important – the link will not work without it.

- In the **mexican** page, click at the very top of the page, then click on the Insert menu and choose Named Anchor. Enter the word 'top' in the Anchor Name box and click OK.

- A small yellow anchor will appear at the top of the page, indicating the place on the page to which the link will jump when clicked.
- Save the page and preview it in the browser to check that the link works.

9 Define a Site

Define a site for Sizzler Sauce and set the index page as the home page. The links will then be displayed in the map view.

Note: In Dreamweaver CS4 you do not need to set the index page as the home page and there is no map view.

10 Images

- Open the image called **chillies.jpg** in PhotoShop 7 and reduce the size to 300 pixels wide (see page 159 for detailed instructions). Save as **chillies_small.jpg**. Open the remaining images in the folder, re-size them to 300 pixels wide in the same way and save them with appropriate new file names.
- Insert the image **chillies_small.jpg** into the index page just below the main heading.
- Make sure you enter Alt text, e.g. chillies.jpg
- Adjust the attributes so that the image appears with no border and aligned to the centre.

11 Tables

Make a table to display a list and images side by side.

- In the **mexican** page, insert a table with two columns and ten rows, and a width of 95%. Set the right-hand column width to 300 pixels.
- Cut and paste the text as appropriate into the table to achieve a good layout, as suggested overleaf, merging rows where necessary.
- Fill the 'chilli con carne' and 'enchilladas' rows with a background colour of your choice and create a new CSS style for the text in those rows, choosing a colour that can be easily read against the background.
- Once you are happy with the layout of the table, you can copy and paste it into the **indian** page, then change the text as appropriate.

12 Insert a Comment

Insert a comment in the **mexican** page to explain the layout of the second table, i.e. that it is the second table, and give the number of rows and columns with today's date.

13 Insert Meta Tags

Insert relevant keywords and description meta tags in the index page.

Suggested Layout of Table on Mexico Page

Mexican Recipes

Chilli Con Carne	
Ingredients:	
500g lean minced beef 1 x 15 oz can red kidney beans 1 x 15 oz can Hot Sizzler chilli sauce 2 large onions, chopped 3 cloves garlic, crushed 1 red pepper 2 tbs tomato purée 2 tsp paprika 1 tsp ground cumin 2 tsp dried marjoram ½ pint beef stock 1 tablespoon oil	Logo
Directions:	
Heat the oil in a large pan and add the onions, cook for about 5 minutes until soft and transparent. Add the red pepper, chilli, paprika and cumin and cook for another couple of minutes, stirring now and again. Then turn the heat up and add the minced beef to the pan. Break up the beef with a spatula and make sure it is browned all over before adding the Sizzler sauce, the beef stock, marjoram and tomato purée. Season with salt and pepper and stir well. Bring to the boil, then turn down the heat so that the sauce is just simmering and cover. Leave for about 20 minutes, adding a little more water if necessary. Drain the kidney beans and add to the sauce with the garlic and cook for a further 10 minutes, again adding more water if necessary. Serve with boiled rice and top with sour cream or Greek yoghurt.	

Graphics Software

The instructions given in this section refer to PhotoShop 7. Where there is a significant difference between PhotoShop 7 and PhotoShop CS4, instructions are given for both versions.

Placing images with large file sizes into web pages increases the download time. This is a great disadvantage as most users will not wait more than a few seconds for a page to download. So it is important that you use images with a small file size in your web pages. Note: size in this case refers to the size of the file in kilobytes and not the physical size of the image in pixels. However, the pixel size does of course affect the number of kilobytes of the file.

Re-sizing Images

> ### Tip
>
> When you are re-sizing images for the Web, remember not to change the height without changing the width exactly in proportion. This is known as the aspect ratio. If this is not maintained, the image will lose quality and become pixellated so that you can clearly see the squares of colour – pixels – that make up the image.
>
> This can also happen when an image has been enlarged and the resolution of the original is not sufficient. It is therefore a good idea to use images with high resolution and then reduce the size and compress them to achieve a good quality image, but with a small file size.

You should only re-size an image using graphics software which can maintain the aspect ratio for you. In the case of PhotoShop this is termed 'Constrain Proportions' (see below).

- Open PhotoShop 7 and open the image you wish to re-size.
- Click on the Image menu and choose Image Size.
- Make sure that the Constrain Proportions and the Resample Image boxes are checked.
- Click the down arrow beside the Width box to specify the width or height either in pixels or as a percentage.
- Enter the required value in the Width box.
- Click OK.
- Click on File and Save As.
- Save the file with a new name, so that the original remains unaltered.
- Close the image. *Important:* when asked to save this file, say No, otherwise you will save over the original file.

Choose pixels or percentage here

Enter the new value for the width here

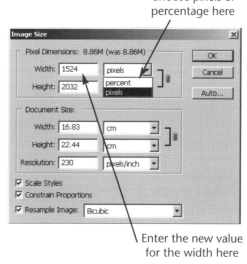

Image File Compression for the Web

The most common image file formats used on the Web are .gif, .jpg and .png (these formats are described fully in the next section). In general, the .gif format is used for drawings, transparencies and animations and the .jpg format is used for photographs where there is a large amount of colour information required. The .png format is still being developed, but is being increasingly used as an alternative to both .jpg and .gif.

Photoshop 7 – .jpg Images

Reduce the size of the image in pixels:

- Open the image in PhotoShop.
- Click on the Image menu and choose Image Size.
- Check that the Constrain Proportions and Resample Image boxes are ticked – this ensures that the aspect ratio will be maintained when the image is resized.
- Enter a width of 300 pixels or less and click OK.

Optimise the image and Save it for the Web – PhotoShop 7:

- Click on the File menu and choose Save for Web.
- Check that the file type is JPEG and set the Compression Quality to High/Medium to achieve a file size of 9Kb or below using the slider in the Quality box.

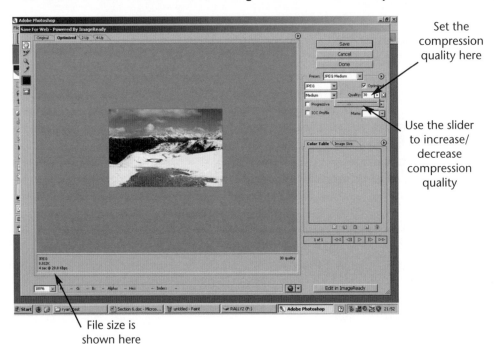

Set the compression quality here

Use the slider to increase/ decrease compression quality

File size is shown here

- Click Save.
- Enter a different name in the File Name box so that both the optimised image and the original image are retained.
- Click Save.
- Close the image.

Important: when asked to save this file, say No, otherwise you will save over the original file.

Optimise the image and save it for the Web – PhotoShop CS4:

- Click on the File menu and choose Save for Web & Devices.
- Check that the file type is JPEG.
- Set the compression quality to high/medium to achieve a file size of 9Kb or less.

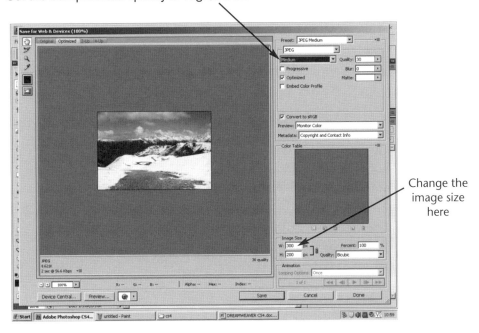

Change the image size here

PhotoShop 7 – gif Images

Because gif image files can only display 256 colours, when optimising these images for use on the Web, lossy compression and/or dithering may be necessary to reduce the file size.

Lossy compression:

- Lossy compression reduces the file size by selectively discarding data – a higher lossy setting results in more data being discarded, and therefore a loss of picture quality.

- File size can often be reduced by 5% to 40% using the lossy option.

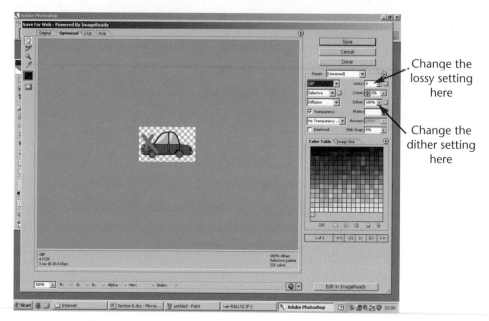

Dithering:

- Dither refers to the method of simulating colours not available in the colour display system of your computer.
- Images with primarily solid colours may work well with no dither.
- Images with continuous-tone colour (especially colour gradients) may require dithering to prevent colour banding.
- Diffusion dither applies a random pattern that is usually less noticeable than pattern dither. The dither effects are extended across adjacent pixels.
- A *higher dither percentage* creates the appearance of more colours and more detail in an image, but can also *increase the file size*.

PhotoShop CS4 – gif Images

Transparency with gif Images

A transparent image allows the page background to display through it so the image appears to have no visible border around it. This is useful when the background of the page is a different colour from the background of the image.

Without transparency, the image will have a border around it, but when saved with transparency the image will appear to float against the page background. Currently the only formats that support transparency are the gif and png formats.

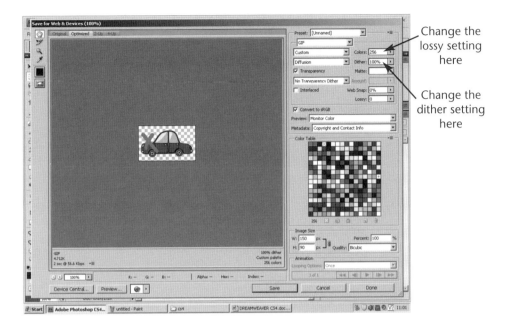

Change the
lossy setting
here

Change the
dither setting
here

Example:

Non-transparent

Transparent

One problem with transparent images is that not all browsers display them properly. Some older browsers cannot distinguish between the GIF87 non-transparent format and the GIF89a transparent format and will display the original background colour. For this reason, graphic artists need to attempt to make the background colour of the image the same as the background colour of the intended page, even if they are saving it in transparent format.

To apply transparency to part of an image:

- Open your image in Adobe PhotoShop.
- Click on File, Save for Web.

Click to select one or more colours here

Click this icon to make the selected colour(s) transparent

- Choose gif as the file type and make sure Transparency is checked.
- Click on the down arrow under Transparency and choose Diffusion Transparency Dither. Then click on the colour you want to make transparent and click on the checkerboard icon at the bottom of the Save for Web Dialogue box. If you wish to make more than one colour transparent at the same time, press the Control key while you click.
- Click on the Transparency icon at the bottom of the Save for Web dialogue box.
- Click Save and your image will be saved with the colour that you selected made transparent.

Note that this method can also be used to *delete* a colour from the image: select the colour and click on the dustbin icon.

Creating Navigation buttons in PhotoShop 7

- Create a new image – click on File, New.
- Set the width to 90 pixels and the height to 40 pixels.

- Using the icons in the Toolbox (see diagram opposite), set the background to transparent and the colour mode to RGB.
- Click OK.
- Change the foreground colour to blue (#0066CC), or a Web-safe colour of your choice.

The Options Toolbar

◆ Note that the options shown in this toolbar show different icons, depending on which tool you select in the Toolbox.

Click the down arrow to change to a different tool

Choose a shape

Click here to see auto shapes

- Click on the Paint Bucket in the Toolbox, hold the mouse down for a second or two and change to the Gradient tool.
- Click and drag diagonally across the rectangle to fill it with a gradient fill – this is now Layer 1.
- To create a 3D effect, click on the Layer Menu, Layer Style and choose Bevel and Emboss. Use the size and depth sliders to create the 3D effect. You can add a drop shadow as well if you wish.
- Click the Text button in the Toolbox.
- The Options Toolbar now changes as below:

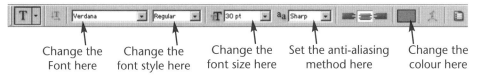

Change the Font here   Change the font style here   Change the font size here   Set the anti-aliasing method here   Change the colour here

- Set the font to Verdana, the size to 12 pts, the colour to dark blue (#003366) and the alignment to centre.
- Click anywhere inside the blue rectangle and type Home. This is now Layer 2.
- If the text does not appear in the centre of the button you can move it with the Move tool in the Toolbox.
- Now save the document as a .psd file (PhotoShop file). Click on File, Save as, and enter the file name as **button.psd**. You will need this document to make further buttons with different text on each.
- Save the image again, this time as **home.gif**, into your **images** folder. In the Indexed Color box, set the Palette to Web and the row order in the gif options box to Interlaced. Click OK.
- To make another button with different text, select the text and type 'Mexico'. Save as **mexico.gif**
- You can now change the text to 'India' and save as **india.gif**
- The original PhotoShop file called **button.psd** remains on screen. Close without saving.

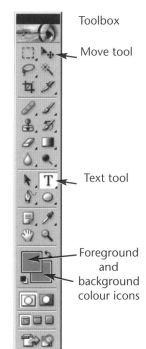

Toolbox

Move tool

Text tool

Foreground and background colour icons

Animating an Image for the Web

Animated cartoons are made up of many drawings of the same image in different positions. So animating an image for the Web requires the production of several different image files, which are then loaded into a graphics application and made into a series of frames, each showing the image in a different way. The delay between each image is then set to create the animated effect.

Creating an Animation Button

Step 1 – Create a layered image:

- First you need to create a button (see separate instructions) or use one from file.
- Open PhotoShop and then open the button file.
- If the Layers palette is not visible, click on Window, Show Layers.
- Create a new layer by clicking on the icon at the bottom of the Layers palette as shown below.

Click on these 'eyes' to make the layers invisible

Click here to create a new layer

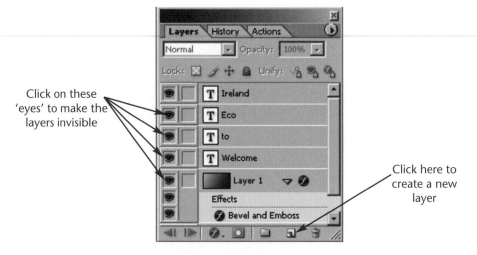

- Select an appropriate colour and font for the text from the Text Options toolbar.
- Click on the Type tool and type 'Welcome'.
- Create a second layer and type 'to'.
- Create a third layer and type 'ECO'.
- Create a fourth layer and type 'Ireland'.
- Save the file as **eco_button.psd**

Step 2 – Create a frame for each layer (PhotoShop 7 only):

- Click on the Jump To button at the bottom of the Toolbox.
- Image Ready will open, with your saved image intact.
- Click on Window, and choose Show Layers and Show Animation to display these panels on your screen.

- The Animation panel now shows one frame containing the entire image with the words displayed on top of one another.
- In the Layers panel, click on the 'eye' beside each text layer to make the words invisible.

Animation panel

New Frame icon

- Now create a second frame by clicking on the New Frame icon in the Animation panel.
- In the Layers palette, click on the eye beside the first text layer – 'Welcome'.
- Create a third frame and click the eye beside the second text layer in the Layers panel – 'to' – and unclick the eye beside the second one, so that only 'to' is visible.
- Repeat this process until only 'Ireland' is visible.
- Your Animation panel should now look like this:

Step 2 – Create a frame for each layer (PhotoShop CS4 only):

- Click on the Window menu, Animation to display the Animation panel.
- Click on the Convert to Frame Animation button at the bottom right of the Animation panel.

- The Animation panel now shows one frame containing the entire image with the words displayed on top of one another.
- In the Layers panel, click on the 'eye' beside each text layer to make the words invisible.
- Now create a second frame by clicking on the New Frame icon in the Animation panel
- In the Layers panel, click on the eye beside the first text layer – 'Welcome'.
- Create a third frame and click the eye beside the second text layer in the Layers panel – 'to' – and unclick the eye beside the second one, so that only 'to' is visible.
- Repeat this process until only 'Ireland' is visible.
- Your Animation panel should now look like this:

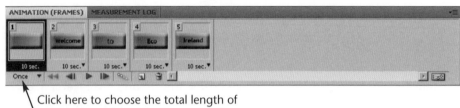

Click here to choose the total length of
the animation (once, forever, etc.)

Step 3 – Set the timing:

- Click on the down arrow underneath each frame to set the delay time between each frame – 1 second is usually about right.
- Click on the Play button to preview the animation. You can adjust the timing if you wish.

Step 4 – Optimise the image (PhotoShop 7):

- Click on the Optimized tab at the top of your active image. The Optimize panel should now be viewable (if it is not, click on Window, Optimize). The default settings are fine for this image. Click on OK.
- Click on File, Save Optimized as **eco_button** – notice the image is now a gif image.
- Close the file.
- The image is now ready for inserting into a web page.

Step 4 – Optimise the image (PhotoShop CS4):

- Click on File, Save for Web & Devices.
- Check that the image type is a gif.
- Click Save.
- Save the file as **eco_button** in the **images** folder of your **website** folder.
- PhotoShop CS4 automatically optimises the image and saves the animation.

File Formats for the Web

Graphics

The most common image file formats are .gif, .jpg and .png. The .png format is still being developed and will be more widely used in the future.

.gif

Gif stands for graphic interchange format. The .gif image format can support only 256 colours as it has an 8-bit palette. Therefore it is more suitable for images with a limited number of colours, such as a hand-drawn image. It supports animation effects and it is also used when transparency is required.

.jpg

JPEG stands for Joint Photographic Experts Group, the organisation that created the format. The .jpg image format can support 16.7 million colours (24-bit colour information), which makes it suitable for photographs. It cannot support animation or transparency.

.png

The PNG (Portable Network Graphics) image format can support 16 million colours. There are different versions:

- PNG-8 is equivalent to a .gif, but has the advantage that its file size is smaller because it saves colours more efficiently. However, PNG-8 is not yet suitable for animations because not all browsers support it, so gifs are still the best option for animation effects.
- PNG-24 is equivalent to a jpg but as the file size is bigger, it is not suitable as an alternative to the jpg at the moment.

Audio

Audio files are very large because they contain a huge amount of data, even more than image files. To prevent slow download times, they need to be compressed. There are three major groups of audio file formats:

- uncompressed audio formats, for example WAV and AIFF
- formats with lossless compression, such as FLAC and WMA Lossless
- formats with lossy compression, such as MP3, ATRAC and lossy WMA.

The most widely used audio file format is now .mp3. This format can compress sound files to one-tenth of their original file size without significant loss of quality and allows them to be downloaded or streamed. Streaming is much more efficient as long as you have a broadband connection.

169

You should be aware that not all audio formats can be played by all plug-in media players. This means that if you insert a sound file into a web page, a visitor to that page will be not be able to hear the sound unless they have the correct plug-in installed on their computer. However, most plug-ins support the .mp3 format.

When inserting a sound file into a web page using Dreamweaver 8, there are two options.

Option 1 – Download and play (create a link to the sound file so that it plays when the link is clicked):

- Type the name of the sound file and highlight it.
- Click the Browse button beside the link box and browse to the sound file.
- Save the file and preview it in the browser.
- Click on the file to hear the sound.

Option 2 – Embed the sound file directly into a web page so that it plays on loading Dreamweaver 8:

- Display the Behaviors panel by choosing Windows/Behaviors.
- Click the + sign in the Behaviors panel and choose Play Sound. The Play Sound dialogue box opens.

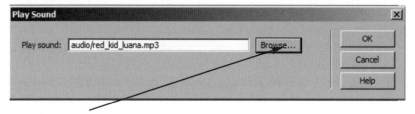

- Click the Browse button to find and select the file.
- Click OK.
- To make sure the behaviour associated with the sound is set to onLoad, click the drop-down arrow on the Events button in the Behaviors panel and choose onLoad from the list.
- Save and preview your page – the sound will play as soon as the sound file has a chance to load. Be aware that there are Web users who find a background sound as irritating as supermarket muzak, and that there are users who browse the Internet with the sound turned off.

Dreamweaver CS4

To embed the sound file directly into a web page so that it plays on loading:

- Click the Insert menu, Media and choose Plugin.
- Browse to the sound file you wish to embed and click OK.

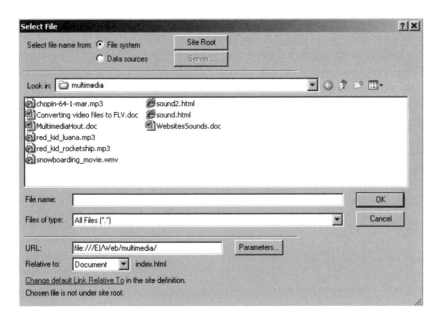

Video

The same problem exists with video files as with audio files, but video files are bigger again. As with audio files, in recent years compressed file formats have been developed which help to overcome this problem. There are also a number of other factors which determine file size, such as the quality of the original video, whether it is black and white or in colour, etc.

There is also a huge number of file types – the advent of digital cameras with video capability and video cameras has added to the range of different file types. Some of the most common ones are:

- .swf (Flash movie)
- .flv (Flash Video file)
- .wmv (Windows Media Video)
- .rm (Real Media file)
- .mpg (MPEG Video file)
- .mp4 (MPEG-4 Video file)

As with audio files, the best way is the download and play method. Simply create a link to the file, so that when it is clicked the video will play.

Also as with audio files, embedding the video directly into the page can cause problems if the relevant plug-in is not installed on the user's computer.

Dynamic HTML

Dynamic HTML (DHTML) allows the Web designer to create interactive and dynamic content in a web page (such as interactive games and animation) without reloading from the Web server.

There are four parts to DHTML:

1 Document Object Model (DOM). This is an interface that allows programs and scripts to update the content, structure and style of documents dynamically. It is independent of platform and language. It ensures that scripts, CSS and XHTML work together in a web page.
2 Scripts – JavaScript and ActiveX are the two most common scripts used to activate DHMTL.
3 Cascading Style Sheets (CSS) allows Web developers to control the style and layout of web pages.
4 XHTML – the X stands for Extensible, which means that the language has been designed so that the user can extend its capabilities. This allows Web designers to create their own objects and tags in their web pages and therefore gives more control over their appearance and functionality.

The two most commonly used functions of DHTML are:

● Changing the tags and attributes. This function allows you to change the attributes of an HTML tag depending on an event outside the browser (e.g. a mouse click, time or date, etc.) A simple example of this code is shown below.
● Real-time positioning. Objects, images and text move around the web page. The user can play interactive games, or portions of the screen can be animated.

Shown below is a simple example of DHTML in a web page using JavaScript.

```
<html>
<head>
```

The JavaScript is entered in the head section of the web page, and this instructs the browser to display either the red ball or the blue ball

```
<script type="text/javascript">
cc=0;
function changeimage()
{
if (cc==0)
{
cc=1;
```

```
document.getElementById('myimage').src= "1blue_ball.gif";
        }
        else
        {
        cc−0;

document.getElementById('myimage').src= "1red_ball.gif";
        }
        }
        </script>
</head>

<body>
        <p align="center">
        <img id="myimage" onclick="changeimage()"
        border="0" src="1red_ball.gif" width= "100" height=
        "100" />
        </p>
        <p align="center">Click to see the blue ball</p>

</body>
</html>
```

Then in the image tag in the body section of the page the browser is instructed to display the red ball until the image is clicked and then change to the blue ball

Click to see the blue ball

Testing your Site

When you have finished creating your website, make sure that you have not made any spelling or grammatical errors. Dreamweaver has a spell check facility (click on the Text Menu and choose Check Spelling, or press Shift and F7).

Check your Filenames

Web hosts have naming conventions for filenames – we learned at the beginning of this section that we should not use any capital letters, spaces or special symbols in web page file names and that the home page of every website should be named index.html. It is all too easy when you are collecting images and creating web pages to forget these conventions. Then you may run into problems when you come to upload your files. So check that every image and web page file name is correct.

Check the Code

If you have created your website in a Web authoring application, you can check the code using its HTML validator (in Dreamweaver, click on the Commands menu and choose Clean up HTML/XML). Click on the options that apply to your page.

If you have created your website using HTML, and you do not have access to a Web authoring application, there a number of software validators on the Web. There are also sites on the Web that can check your code remotely.

You can also check the code yourself using the following guidelines.

Eliminate Errors

- Check that all HTML code is correctly specified, e.g. the colour attribute is spelled the American way – as in <color>.
- Ensure that all HTML tags use the correct syntax. Check for missing quotation marks, for attribute values and missing tag angled brackets or unnecessary single brackets.
- Check that opening HTML tags have corresponding closing tags (unless they are stand-alone tags, in which case check that there is a forward slash before the closing right-angled bracket).
- Check that all URLs, both local and remote, are correctly specified.
- Make sure that all nested tags are in the correct order – remember, the first tag opened should be the last tag closed.

Validate the Links

Pages on the Web are constantly changing, so it is a good idea to double check for links which are no longer live, or that go to the wrong page. If you have remote links to websites outside your site on your pages, connect to the Internet so that you can click on each link to make sure it goes to the right website/web page. If you are using Dreamweaver, first open the page you wish to check, then click on the File menu, Check Page and choose Check Links. If there are any broken links, these will be listed at the bottom of the window.

Check your Pages in Different Browsers

You must test your work in at least two different browsers – Microsoft's Internet Explorer and Mozilla Firefox are two examples. They render pages differently, and your page must look right in both. There are other browsers, such as Opera, Safari and Google Chrome, and it is a good idea to check in a third browser. Most browsers can be downloaded free from the Internet.

Check your Pages at Different Screen Resolutions

Most monitors have a default resolution of 1024 x 768 pixels. However, some screens can have a resolution of 800 x 600, or 1290 x 1024. The following points should be checked at each resolution size:

- Can users see all the information on the page at all resolutions, without scrolling?
- If scrolling is necessary, is all the critical information on the page visible?
- When looking at the page at lower or higher resolutions, are all the elements, such as tables and images, still lined up correctly?

To change the screen resolution:

- Close all programs.
- Click on Start, Control Panel, and choose Display.
- In the Display dialogue box, click on the Settings tab and use the slider to change the resolution.
- Click Apply – the screen will go black for a few seconds and then the new resolution will be applied.

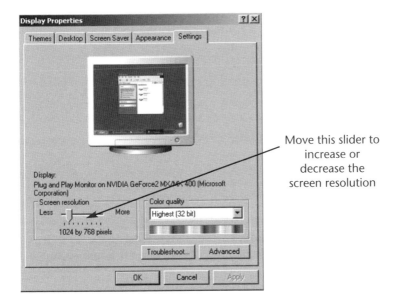

Move this slider to increase or decrease the screen resolution

Choosing a Web Host

When you have finally finished testing your website, the next step is to upload it onto the Web server. A Web server is a remote computer which has the software capability of delivering pages to a browser. There are many Web hosting companies on the Web. Generally, the larger hosts tend to offer faster servers and better bandwidths. There are also many sites which review Web hosts and give top ten or top 100 ratings, such as:

- www.webhostingsearch.com/
- www.webhostinggeeks.com/
- www.uk.answers.yahoo.com/

If you are not sure about your requirements, it is a good idea to telephone the Web host to discuss your needs. These are a few questions you might ask:

- **Access speed.** Does the host offer good download speeds at all times of the day? This can depend on the hard drive, memory and processing speed of the Web server. Bandwidth (the amount of data that can be sent through a channel or network) is also a factor. If the server is handling a large amount of traffic, access can be slow.
- **Web space.** First check the total size of the files in your website in megabytes and then ask how much Web space is being offered. You may wish to expand your site in the future, so will the Web host give you more space when you need it and will that increase the cost?
- **Cost.** How much is the rental for Web space? A general rule is that the more you pay, the more control you will have on what appears on your pages. You may have to carry advertising, particularly if the Web space is either free or very cheap. This advertising may not be appropriate for your site, and may also slow down access speed.
- **Restrictions.** Are there any restrictions on the type of content accepted?
- **Regulations.** Examine the rules, e.g. naming conventions, and then check that your site conforms to these rules.
- **Contact and technical support.** Can you contact your Web host quickly if you have a problem, and do they respond to email immediately?

You also need to decide on a Web address with a domain name. It is advisable to choose a top-level domain name such as .com, .net or .org because most people are familiar with these and they are easier to remember than more obscure ones (which are of course cheaper). Then include the name of your company, club, etc. and/or the topic of your website. You will need several different versions of your Web address, as there may be other sites already registered with the same name.

Once you have decided on a host, read the rules and regulations on their website before filling in the form and signing up.

Uploading your Web Pages

Through the Browser

The simplest way to upload web pages to the Internet is to use Internet Explorer. This method does not require any special software to be installed. In the address bar of Internet Explorer, type your Web host's ftp address, wait for the dialogue box to appear and then fill in your username and password. Once you're logged in, copy and paste the files from your computer and they will be uploaded and appear on the Internet.

> However, be warned that there are security implications with this method, and the files on your computer may be at risk.

Using FTP (File Transfer Protocol)

You will need access to an FTP client. There are many open source FTP clients available as free downloads (such as FileZilla, Classic FTP). You should have already checked whether your host has rules about naming files. Make sure that your website complies with these rules. Then open the FTP program and log on to your site with the following information (which your Web host supplies):

- site address
- username
- password.

Once you have logged on, and connected to the server, a window appears which is very similar to a file management program. The left-hand panel should show your website files stored on your computer and the right-hand panel should show the parent folder on the host's Web server. Then transfer the files by simply copying them over to the remote server. If you have followed the rules, kept your file sizes to a minimum and your files have the correct folder structure, the website will upload quickly.

Uploading Web Pages with Dreamweaver

- Make a site in Dreamweaver for your website folder and files.
- Click on the Site menu and choose Manage Sites.
- Select your site's name in the list of sites and click the Edit button.
- Select the Advanced tab and choose Remote Info.
- Click the down arrow in the Access box and choose FTP.

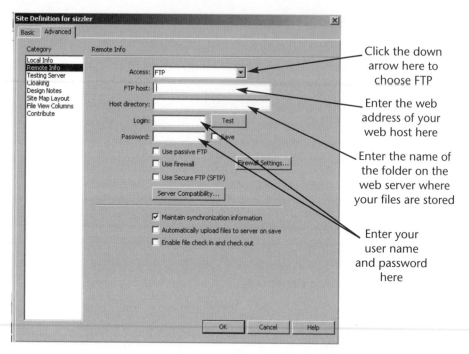

Click the down arrow here to choose FTP

Enter the web address of your web host here

Enter the name of the folder on the web server where your files are stored

Enter your user name and password here

Note: Dreamweaver uses the term 'put' when referring to uploading files on to a server. To upload your files:

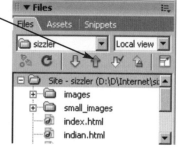

- Click on the Put icon in the Files panel, or you can access the Put command through the Site menu.
- A dialogue box appears asking if you wish to put the whole site up to the server. Click OK.
- When the files are uploaded, a message will appear at the bottom of the Files panel indicating that the files have been successfully uploaded.

Whichever method you choose, once the site has been uploaded, open your browser, enter the address of your website in the address box and press Enter to see your website live on the Internet. Then check that it is displaying correctly. Check it in at least one more browser.

Publicising your Site

Register with a Search Engine

Before registering, you need to find the exact category that your site fits into. Charges vary, and commercial sites may be more expensive. Two websites which offer advice on registering with search engines are:

- http://www.wordsinarow.com/wheretogo.html
- http://www.joyvill.ca/faq-website-search-engine-listing.html

Major Search Engines

Google	Lycos
Yahoo!	Alltheweb
Ask Jeeves	Aol Search
Alta Vista	HotBot
Euroseek	Bing
LookSmart	MSN Search
Ask.com	WebCrawler

Information on these search engines and more can be found at:
http://searchenginewatch.com

Mutual Linking

This is where you contact a website on a similar topic to your own and offer to place a link on your pages to their site, suggesting that they do the same for you. Unless your site is commercial and is in direct competition, this can have the benefit of increasing awareness among users of both sites.

Web Rings

These are websites which have a common theme, and are connected into a circle of mutual links where each site has a common navigation bar.

Discussion Forums

These have sections where you can advertise at no charge; and you can get advice and help from other members.

Maintaining your Site

- Re-assess your design from time to time – Web technology changes quickly, enabling new design features to be used. So check other websites to see what is new, and don't get left behind.
- Expand your site – add new features such as a feedback form, online purchasing, videos, animation, etc.
- The Web changes minute by minute. Check regularly for dead links, remove them and replace with live ones.

- Information may need updating; for example, if you have a site for a football team, you need to update the results page after every match.

Resources

www.w3schools.ie
www.w3c.org
www.webmonkey.com
www.free2use-it.com/
freephotoshop.org
www.lonelyplanet.com/mexico
www.lonelyplanet.com/india
filezilla-project.org/
www.learnwebdevelopment.com/
www.nchsoftware.com/
David Sawyer McFarland, *Dreamweaver 8: The Missing Manual*, O'Reilly Media/ Pogue Press.
Rachel Andrews, *Build Your Own Standards Compliant Website Using Dreamweaver 8*, available from www.sitepoint.com/books/ as a download only (not available as a hard copy).
Janine Warner, *Dreamweaver 8 for Dummies*.
Alan Dillon, *Step by Step Web Design* (currently out of print).
Richard Tammadge, *Web Design* (currently out of print)

Glossary

Acronym The Encarta Dictionary defines an acronym as 'a word formed from the initials or other parts of several words'.

Address book The address book is an essential component of any e-mail system. The Windows Live Mail address book allows you to save comprehensive personal data for an individual.

ADSL (Asymmetric Digital Subscriber Line) A broadband connection that uses the existing telephone copper wire which connects your house to the exchange.

Backbone The backbone of the Internet is the trunk routes – cables, etc. – that carry Internet traffic across oceans and continents.

Bandwidth The speed of an Internet connection. Measured in bits per second (Bps).

Bits per second (Bps) Speed on the Internet is measured in bits per second.

Blog A personal Web journal – short for Web log.

Broadband connection A broadband Internet connection is characterised by being fast (in comparison with dial-up) and is normally always on. Broadband uses various methods or technologies to connect to the Internet.

Browser A client application that allows you to view web pages which can include text, graphics, audio content and videos.

Cache A temporary storage space which your browser uses to save a copy or a snapshot of a web page.

Chat rooms A virtual room on the Internet, where many people can chat to many other people simultaneously, usually on a specific topic or range of topics, e.g. sport, business, science, art, law, etc. Some chat rooms allow you to upload images and music and use voice communication.

Client A client is a software application which is on your computer. It requests information from a server software program which is held on the server's computer.

Contention ratio A measure of how many other users are sharing the same telephone line or cable.

Cookies Small text files that are downloaded to your hard disk by certain websites when you visit them. These cookies can come from the websites themselves or from the advertisements that appear in a website. They can be used to keep track of your browsing activity. Some expire when you shut down your computer, and others remain on your hard disk drive.

Dial-up connection The most basic type of connection. It uses the existing land line telephone system.

Digital certificate An electronic ID file operating like a driver's licence or passport. It is an electronic version of an ID card or passport, issued by a trusted, independent organisation (a Certificate Authority) such as Alpha Trust, VeriSign, etc. It is used to authenticate the validity of a website.

Digital signatures Many commercial e-mail clients can use a digital signature to sign e-mail messages. A digital signature provides signer and document authentication.

Dithering Dithering refers to the method of simulating colours now available in the colour display system of your computer.

Domain names The domain name system is fundamental to the operation of the Internet. www.rte.ie is the domain name for the RTE website; the sub-domain is rte and the upper domain is .ie.

Domain name server The server that translates host names into IP numbers.

Download The transfer of data from one computer to another.

E-mail (electronic mail) Mail that is sent over the Internet: one of the most important uses of the Internet.

E-mail client program To send an e-mail, as opposed to Web e-mail, you need an e-mail client program installed on your computer, e.g. Outlook 2003 or Outlook 2007.

E-mail etiquette (netiquette) The etiquette appropriate for use on the Internet. It is a matter of being considerate, aware and careful when sending an e-mail.

Emoticons (combination of the words 'emotion' and 'icon'). Emoticons are defined in the Encarta Dictionary as 'an arrangement of keyboard characters intended to convey an emotion, usually viewed sideways'. Emoticons are also known as 'smileys'.

Encryption A means of converting information using a code that prevents it being understood by anyone who isn't authorised to view data.

Ethernet LAN A wired network – computers are connected together with cables (as distinct from wirelessly).

Favourites/Favorites When you find a site or web page of particular interest, its URL can be saved as a 'Favorite' (Internet Explorer) or Bookmark (Firefox).

File A computer file can be a program, an image, a video or a document stored on a computer.

File transfer protocol (FTP) A set of rules that govern the transmission of files from one computer to another over the Internet.

Filtering/content control software Used to block access to websites which may be deemed inappropriate or objectionable.

Filters You can define filters or rules which tell your e-mail client to direct new mail to particular folders.

Firewalls A firewall is a system designed to protect your computer from an attack from an intruder. It prevents unauthorised access to or from a network, or from a personal computer. It can be hardware or software, or a combination of both.

Folders In Windows files are grouped or organised in folders. The paper analogy is a piece of paper in a cardboard folder. This arrangement allows you to organise and locate files on a hard disk. When files are bundled and compressed into a special type of folder, the files are said to be zipped and the folder is a zip folder.

Frequently asked questions (FAQ) Documents that answer questions on commonly requested information.

Graphic interchange format (.gif) An image file format used on the Web for animated and transparent images and also for images with a small number of colours.

GUI (Graphical User Interface) GUI (pronounced 'gooey') allows users to interact with their computer by using a mouse to point and click on an icon on the computer screen. This action causes the computer to launch a program, open an e-mail or execute some such other predefined command.

Hash algorithm Essentially, hashing algorithms generate a nearly unique number, or hash, from a set of data, such as a file, message or phrase. The algorithm must ensure that creating another message that has the same hash is extremely difficult. This property plays an important role in the process of digital message signing. (Source: http://tech.mit.edu/V129/N31/rivestmd6.html.)

Home page A pre-set start page which opens in your browser window.

HTML (HyperText Markup Language) The language used to create web pages.

HTTP (HyperText Transfer Protocol) The protocol that delivers web pages which have been requested to your browser. It is a request/response system.

IM (Instant Messaging) The exchange of text messages through a software application in real time.

IMAP4 (Internet Message Access Protocol) IMAP4 is very similar to a POP3 server, but this protocol allows you to view your e-mails without downloading them to your computer. You must delete your e-mails from the server.

IP (Internet Protocol) The protocol responsible for the address component of data packets sent from one computer to another over a network or networks.

IP address To access the Internet every connection needs a unique address – an IP address. An IP address is 32 bits long, it is broken into four parts and each part is separated by a dot. For example 89.207.56.140 is the decimal representation of the binary code for a particular IP address, in this case www.rte.ie.

ISP (Internet service provider) Provides access to the Internet. Most ISPs are telecommunications companies.

JPEG (Joint Photographic Experts Group) (.jpg) The most used file format for graphic files on the Internet.

Kilobits per second (Kpbs) The standard measurement used to describe the transfer speed of data on the Internet.

LAN (Local Area Network) A network that has been established in a home, office or school building.

Latency The delay in the transmission of a signal.

Links A link provides a connection to another document or file.

Links bar The links bar is used to store the address of the websites you visit most often.

Lossy compression Lossy compression reduces the size of a file by discarding surplus data.

Mailboxes A mailbox is where your mail is held on the server.

Mailing list An e-mail based notice distribution mechanism or a discussion group.

Modem (modulator/demodulator) A device that allows a computer to communicate with another computer through a telephone line. It converts the computer's digital signal into an analogue signal.

MP3 A compressed music format.

Network A network occurs when you connect two or more computers together so that they can share resources.

Network control protocol (NCP) Allows host computers to talk to each other within a network.

Network interface card (NIC) The task of the NIC card is to convert a computer's internal stream of data into a form that can be transmitted over a network and vice versa.

Outlook A business e-mail client program developed by Microsoft.

Packet When you transfer data on the Internet, the data is broken into packets; these packets contain the address of where the data came from and where it is going.

Phishing A means whereby personal information (e.g. credit card and account details) are obtained by fraudulent means.

.png (portable network graphic) A graphics file format that is being increasingly used for the Web, but is not yet fully developed.

POP3 (post office protocol) client A POP3 client (server) downloads all mail to the client computer (i.e your computer), and removes it from the server. Most ISPs use this server. Your incoming mail is held on the server's computer and when you check your mail, the mail is then transferred to your computer.

Protocol Refers to a set of rules that define the way you communicate on the Internet. Internet protocols standards are defined in RFC documents.

RealAudio A standard for streaming compressed audio over the internet.

RFC (request for comments) Proposals published by the Internet Engineering Task Force. The proposals relate to the Internet and its workings.

Router/residential gateway Provides a link between your computer/LAN and the Internet. It directs the traffic between your computer and the Internet.

RSS feeds RSS stands for 'really simple syndication' or 'rich site summary'. It is used to update frequently accessed digital content such as news and podcasts.

Save as Type formats – Web pages

- Webpage, complete (*htm; *html) saves all the files necessary to display the page in their original format. The web page is saved as a separate file and a folder is created to store the graphics, etc.

- Web Archive, single file (*mht) saves all the information, including graphics, as a single file.

- Webpage, HTML only (*htm; *html) saves the text on the page but not the graphics or other files. If the web pages contain frames, it will not save each frame. (Frames are separate areas in a web page that act in a similar way to a single page.)

- Text File (*.txt) Saves the text as plain text without any formatting. The contents of frames are not saved.

Search Engines Searches for information entered into a search field. The relevant information is then retrieved from a vast database to which a particular search engine has access. The information is then displayed in the search engine web page.

SMS (short message service) A mechanism for delivering short messages over mobile networks.

SMTP (simple mail transfer protocol) The protocol used to send an e-mail over the Internet.

Spam Unsolicited e-mail. Spammers may suggest, for example, that you have been specially chosen as the winner of an exciting exotic foreign holiday.

Spyware Collects private information without the knowledge or consent of the person whose information is being collected and uses the victim's own Internet bandwidth to transmit the information.

SSL (Secure Sockets Layer) Uses a complex system of key exchanges between your browser and the server you are communicating with in order to encrypt data *before* transmitting it across the Web.

Streaming The process whereby you listen to or watch content almost instantaneously as it is downloaded/received.

Tabs – Internet Explorer Tabs allow a user to open different web pages in the one browser window.

TCP/IP Protocol (Transmission Control Protocol/Internet Protocol) The TCP/IP is the primary protocol that governs the Internet. The TCP manages the disassembling of, and reassembling of, data packets, which are then brought back to their original data format. It is also responsible for the retransmission of lost packets. TCP communicates with the host application on one computer and the host application on another computer on a network or networks. (Source: http://www.search networking.techtarget.com/sDefinition/)

TLS (Transport Layer Security) A protocol used to establish a secure connection between a client and a server.

Trojan horse A virus that masks itself as something desirable. It can destroy files or change data.

Twitter A free service that lets you keep in touch with people through the exchange of short messages.

Upload The transfer of data from one computer to another.

URL (Uniform Resource Locator) Each website has its own unique address, referred to as a Uniform Resource Locator (URL).

Usenet newsgroups Usenet is one of the oldest communications systems available on the Internet. It was developed to allow people to discuss topics of interest through the medium of text messages or 'posts'.

Virus A malicious code that can delete files from a hard disk or display messages or install unrequested software on your computer.

VoIP (Voice over Internet Protocol) Allows you to make telephone calls using the Internet.

Web mail Web mail is accessed through your browser. The advantage of this option is that your e-mails are stored on your Web browser's server and can be read from any computer with Internet access.

Wireless A wireless connection uses radio waves, so you don't need wires – but you will need a wireless router and each computer needs a wireless network card.

World Wide Web (WWW) Part of the Internet. Specifically, the World Wide Web is a collection of web pages.

Worms Worms come via e-mail. If opened, they replicate themselves and then send themselves to everyone in your address book.

Index